INNER OUT

A Spiritual Journey

Stephanie Klumpp

BALBOA.
PRESS

A DIVISION OF HAY HOUSE

Balboa Press books may be ordered through booksellers or by contacting:

Balboa Press
A Division of Hay House
1663 Liberty Drive
Bloomington, IN 47403
www.balboapress.com
1 (877) 407-4847

Because of the dynamic nature of the Internet, any web addresses or
links contained in this book may have changed since publication and
may no longer be valid. The views expressed in this work are solely those
of the author and do not necessarily reflect the views of the publisher,
and the publisher hereby disclaims any responsibility for them.

The author of this book does not dispense medical advice or prescribe
the use of any technique as a form of treatment for physical, emotional,
or medical problems without the advice of a physician, either directly
or indirectly. The intent of the author is only to offer information
of a general nature to help you in your quest for emotional and
spiritual well-being. In the event you use any of the information in
this book for yourself, which is your constitutional right, the author
and the publisher assume no responsibility for your actions.

Any people depicted in stock imagery provided by Thinkstock are
models, and such images are being used for illustrative purposes only.
Certain stock imagery © Thinkstock.

Print information available on the last page.

ISBN: 978-1-5043-7093-6 (sc)
ISBN: 978-1-5043-7092-9 (e)

Balboa Press rev. date: 12/09/2016

Dedicated to the wounded inner child in all of us.

Introduction

I first heard I was going to write a book in January 2012 while in Las Vegas celebrating my son's twenty-first birthday. We were all walking into a casino when I turned to my left and saw a sign that read *Psychic Readings*. I felt immediately drawn to the area.

Everyone else in our group of seven continued forward, attracted to the lights, bells, and whistles of the casino. The sights and sounds were mesmerizing them and calling them like sirens on the bank of the ocean.

I felt irritated at the noise and the constant message I heard in the cacophony of allure ... *Give me your money ... I have nothing to offer you but an empty feeling of failure and remorse.* I hate gambling. The trip wasn't my idea, but since we had gone to Vegas two years earlier for my daughter's twenty-first birthday, I, in good spirit, went along because I wanted to celebrate with my son.

But I digress. I went to the psychic, whose name was Arkania, and she told me I was going to write a book.

What? Me? What in the world would I write about? I don't know anything. I don't even know how to write well, I thought. I flunked English 101 in college and had to retake it. I'm forever placing too many commas in my sentences and usually allow them to run on.

At that time, the news was a shock, as I felt I did not have a creative bone in my body. Nevertheless, here I am writing a book about my life and my personal journey to spiritual enlightenment and conscious living.

This book is intended to touch those who have or are still battling with alcohol addiction, have low self-worth, and are interested in or already on a path to spiritual growth and living. My training and expertise have come from my fifty-plus years of life. My desire is to bring my authentic *inner* essence *out* into the world by connecting with the expanding collective group of people who know there is more to life and are searching for answers.

You're not going to see a bunch of flowcharts or bulleted lists or other scientific-caliber research material in this book. This book is just an honest story of how I went from living unconsciously, being asleep, and totally unaware of anything bigger than myself or the space I inhabited to a spiritual being who has taught herself how to be happy and live in the present moment.

The information contained in this book is what I've gathered along my journey from my own thoughts and some of what others have told me. In spots I relay some esoteric knowledge I've gleaned from the spirit realm.

Incidentally, the only thing in the writing arena I felt I had going for me was I was related to Harry Gilroy. Uncle Harry was my maternal great-uncle, a former foreign correspondent and cultural news reporter. He was on the staff of the *New York Times* for twenty-one years in the early to mid-1900s, and he also covered native stories such as the Lindbergh kidnapping.

It's interesting in hindsight when you realize you have always been following the breadcrumbs you previously left for yourself without even knowing there was such a system in place (I'm referring to reincarnation and pre-life planning in the spirit world).

Optimistically, at some point along your journey, you begin to realize you are the creator of your life. Life doesn't just happen *to* you. Rather, you vibrationally draw to you the necessary experiences for your own individual growth and expansion, thereby willingly assisting in the expansion of those in and around you in life.

This is my story.

In the Beginning

It's got to happen inside first.
—Jim Morrison

I was born in Erie, Pennsylvania, in 1964. My parents moved my brother and me to Worthington, Ohio, when I was two months old. We were middle class, neither rich nor poor. My parents divorced when I was around seven or eight years old. I always felt connected to God when I was very young; however, my mother's chosen religion ex-communicated her because my father left her, they got divorced, and we stopped going to church.

It never made sense why a place of worshiping God would abandon a person in their darkest hour of need. Mom never went to any church again, although I practically begged her to take me to one over a several-year period. We tried a couple from different denominations but never went more than once. Any reference to God or church was quickly rebuked by my mother and, following in her footsteps, my older brother.

It reminds me of a time when I was about six years old and I had just gotten out of a dental checkup. I had no cavities for the first time I could remember; I almost always had cavities and a lot of them. I jumped into the backseat of Mom's Ford Galaxy 500 and announced, in proud fashion, to my mother and brother who were in the front seat that I knew I wasn't going to have any cavities this time because God told me so!

Well ... I quickly learned that wasn't the right thing to say. My mom stayed silent, not reacting, and my brother snickered and laughed so hard at me I was humiliated into never saying anything about God again. This lasted for about thirty-one years. The tone was essentially, *we don't believe you, and what you say doesn't matter anyway. Shut up, you silly little girl.*

You see, my brother was five years older than me, and an eleven-year-old is God to a six-year-old little girl. *Oh well, I'll just be really good at everything I do from now on,* I told myself.

Within a year after the divorce, my mom fell in love with and ended up marrying a man who was our neighbor in 1972, and they stayed together for thirty-four years until her death following her three-and-a-half-year-long battle with metastatic breast cancer.

My stepfather had four children, three boys and a girl, a dog and a cat and was going through a divorce of his own. I was thrilled at the prospect of gaining a sister and three brothers, an adorable border collie with a limp, named Frisky, and a cat that seemed to just keep on having litters of cute little kittens. This was 1972 when spaying and neutering your pet was not the norm.

I already idolized my soon-to-be big sister who was five years older than me. All six kids were between the ages of eight and fourteen. I had known my new older sister as a neighborhood kid and looked up to her. She was beautiful, and she was going to be my big sister. Words could not describe my excitement.

I got decent grades in school, B average, and was told I was going to college by my biological father and mother. It's funny (funny queer not funny ha-ha) because I don't recall any of my other five siblings being told they definitively were going to go to college. No one asked me. It was a given or a mandate, depending on your perspective.

I suppose it was because I got the best grades out of all my siblings. I graduated from a fairly reputable high school with a 3.1 GPA.

You see, I unwittingly felt touted as somewhat of a family hero due to my desire to be the best in many instances. The problem with this is no one really likes the hero, and I always kind of felt that, and it made me defensive. Family heroes can be viewed as showoffs, and it never really felt like a good thing. It may look good from the outside looking in, but the reality was it always felt like more of a burden or mandate placed on me than a choice I had made for myself. It always felt devoid of consideration for my best and highest good—or hell, just giving me the common consideration and respect to check in and ask me what I wanted for my life. Every decision was made for me from this perspective. I made it my job to comply with those decisions. Life was just easier that way.

I remember once getting all As in eighth grade and my parents making a major announcement out of it at the dinner table one night. They conducted it like a ceremony. They made a speech to all six kids about how everyone should be more like me and get good grades, and then they handed me a one-hundred-dollar bill.

This was 1977, and one hundred dollars was a lot of money for a thirteen-year-old. I was the second to the youngest of the six kids, and my younger stepbrother was only six months younger than me. We were virtual twins in chronological years.

The resentment from my siblings that night was palpable, and it seemed to carry over into all aspects of my life, or at least it appeared that way from my perspective. Things came easy for me. I don't know why; they just did. I was a "good girl," and it was very important to me to please my parents and teachers and anyone else who had authority over me for that matter. I had no self-esteem of my own, and this was how I garnered it, through the approval of others. I was trained from the start.

What is self-esteem anyway? Who knows? What does it mean? It seems like such a buzzword or catch phrase or some new age jargon. Self-esteem is the basic feel of comfort in one's own skin. It is the overall satisfaction with the self.

According to Dictionary.com, self-esteem is "confidence in one's own worth or abilities; self-respect" or "a favorable impression of oneself."

Yeah, I didn't have any of that. I manufactured it by pleasing others. When I got positive feedback, it fed into my self-worth.

It's funny because now it makes sense why I never had self-esteem. I was always held under the microscope concerning my abilities or worth by my parents. Every single thing I did, said, or thought was criticized by someone daily to the point it was nearly impossible to rise above it and see my own inherent worth.

Being one of the youngest of six kids, I always felt like I had something to prove. I never felt seen for who I was. Everyone drank a lot in our family. We drank a lot and covered it up by assuming an outward appearance of perfection.

Alcohol was the method of choice for dealing with emotion. Expression of emotion wasn't encouraged in our family. Emotions were stifled unless and until one introduced alcohol. It was then that the overflow of repressed emotion would come streaming out in the form of effusive affection and clinginess when inebriated. Or worse, occasional screaming and hitting or pontificating about how one must behave in order to be worth anything.

Hitting was not out of the question when one was upset. There were not a lot of *I love you's* during the sober hours. So, you learned not to trust the *I love you's* because they were during drunken moments only and never repeated when sober. Trust in oneself is also compromised as a by-product of living within circumstances of excessive alcohol use.

Nonetheless, we looked like *The Brady Bunch*. In fact, we were often referred to as such.

One can end up having a hard time functioning in a normal and healthy fashion when alcohol is abused by not only the heads of the household but, at differing points, almost all the teenage children as well. Although I recognize some individuals can be raised under these circumstances and not abuse alcohol, that was not the case with me. I emulated the behavior due to my incessant need to fit in and be considered a member of the family unit.

I wanted to be a good girl.

This isn't a book designed to trash my parents or stepparent, because they undoubtedly were doing their best at the time and inadvertently repeating what they had learned early on in their formative years from their own parents. I'm merely setting up the picture of my formative years from my perspective. I also have very few memories of my life when my biological parents were married, from birth to seven years old.

5

I've seen many children who come from families who drink like this and not become alcoholics. However, this was not the case with me. Rather, these circumstances created the perfect storm for me to eventually have a real problem with alcohol. I come from a long lineage of alcoholism on both my mother and biological father's side. I never met my maternal grandmother, as she died from alcohol-related issues at forty years old when my mother was twelve.

Familial dysfunction is a generational, cyclical phenomenon that demands interruption in order for the cycle to be broken. Every family has some kind of dysfunction to overcome. However, as in my case, unless someone in the family stops being overly critical or stops with the self-deprecation and anesthetization, the cycle will continue. On and on it will go, nothing changing, like an ingrained illness. It then gets imprinted into the biological DNA and RNA structures of our generational bloodline unless and until someone says, "Stop! Enough! I cannot participate in the sickness any longer."

Two children from the same household can be screamed at all while growing up, and one will need therapy, and the other will be just fine. In my case, six kids can be raised in a household with alcohol as a central focus, and some will become alcoholics, and some may not drink at all. It depends on the individual emotional sensitivities, intellect, central nervous system makeup, personality, soul characteristics, choices they make in their own adult lives, and the biggest one … what circumstances the particular soul came here to experience. What you are experiencing in life, rest assured, is exactly what you intended. It's all okay.

At thirteen, I started drinking regularly. I would babysit and have friends come over, and we would make suicides. A suicide is where you pour a little (or a lot) of every kind of booze available into a mason jar and top it off with whatever mix was readily available at the time, be it juice, cola, tea, or all three. They tasted like turpentine—not that I've tried turpentine, but I'm quite sure if I did, it would remind me of my childhood suicide days.

I drank to intoxication nearly every weekend from my sophomore year in high school until graduation. By the time I went to college, my drinking habit was in full swing. My drinking grew to four nights and/or days (on average) a week to the point of intoxication, regurgitation, and/or passing out until my graduation. I was hung over nearly half of my early life. If I wasn't drinking, I was hung over from the excess of it. I held the dubious honor of being the best beer chugger at college. That title was tested nearly every time I went to a bar or party and some huge guy would want to challenge me. I always won.

Great, huh? Really something to be proud of. It's a wonder I managed to graduate. But I did.

I received a bachelor's of science degree in criminal justice and was hired by a large law enforcement agency about three months postgraduation, in spite of my pending OMVI—operating a motor vehicle while under the influence of drugs and/or alcohol charge.

The philosophy, I assume, was that I didn't yet have a conviction, so it was okay to hire me. I am forever grateful for that fateful decision.

Alcohol was my drug of choice, specifically beer, for a solid twenty years, on the regular. I'm positive I would have had more drunk-driving charges but for the extension of "professional courtesy." I was pulled over a couple times while drunk and let go. Professional courtesy is where a law enforcement officer doesn't charge another law enforcement officer, or in some cases family of law enforcement officers, for a traffic offense in recognition of being one of his/her own. It is virtually nonexistent in today's society and rightfully so, in my opinion. Society demanded that it change, and for the most part, it has.

I never thought I would be able to quit drinking. I couldn't picture my life without booze (beer) or the ability to numb out. I was petrified to feel my way through life. I had gotten so used to my pattern of drinking until I got drunk, vomiting that night or the next morning so I could go to work, taking a day off from drinking, and starting all over again the following day. That was my pattern. Get drunk. Be deathly ill the next day. Get rest. Feel good the following morning and start all over again, every other day for years and years.

My life was sickeningly exhausting.

Law Enforcement Career

Nearly all men can stand adversity, but if you
want to test a man's character, give him power.
—Abraham Lincoln

I met and got engaged to my boss, my sergeant, shortly
after I was hired by a large law enforcement agency. By
shortly, I mean three months. I was twenty-two years old.
We got married a year and a half later. I got pregnant with
my first child two months after getting married and had
two children by the time I was twenty-seven.

Remember when I said I didn't want to disappoint
anyone in a position of authority over me? My aim was
to please. I was a pleaser. I was on the fast track. I fast-
tracked everything.

And remember I was the hero? Heroes have to stay
ahead of the game; if not, then God forbid you're no longer
the hero. Then what? Well, I was too afraid to find out.

I got promoted to corporal after being in the department
for five years. Ten years into my career, I was promoted to
the rank of sergeant, transferred to a completely different
building, and met a woman who worked for me. We

immediately fell in love. I was blindsided and subsequently blown away by feelings I had never experienced with someone of the same gender. There was a force inside of me in the form of extreme desire that catapulted me into the next level of my life. This same force led me to make a decision that was necessary, but under normal circumstances, I wouldn't have been able to make it, due to my now-ingrained proclivity to sheer obedience to what was expected of me.

I was outed within the law enforcement agency where I worked, and I left my husband. At the time (1997), there were no openly gay cops in any agency, so it was an inadvertent favor, as I'm sure I would not have had the ability at that time to do it for myself, at least not in the beginning.

My being thrust into embracing my homosexuality in the workplace, walking proudly and not running from it, enabled many homosexuals from several agencies to come out. I was plunged into being openly gay and trying to wrap my head around the whole idea of being a homosexual, not because I felt it was wrong but because I had been trained by society that it was wrong. In my heart, the only thing I was feeling was, how could a love such as this be wrong?

I began to learn to live in the truth of who I am. In hindsight, I now know that was the first inkling that my soul was trying to wake me up.

At thirty-three years old, I moved to an apartment and began a whole new life for myself. This time it was my choice, on my terms, for the first time in my life. I was following my inner guidance and seeking my personal road to freedom and happiness. It was extremely scary. She and I eventually moved in together.

Meanwhile, I was engaged in a custody battle, yet I kept drinking, knowing it was hurting my chances of getting my kids. I just didn't feel I could stop. I didn't feel worthy. I wasn't good enough. I was doing what I wanted to do and not following the previously set protocol by my mother, consisting of a white picket fence, 2.5 children, and a standard fairy-tale relationship.

Besides, in hindsight, I believe I was thinking if I lost custody of my children, I could always blame it on the booze and not have to look at my own poor behavior with equally poor choices.

I deeply loved my kids and never believed I would lose them. God knew I loved them with everything in me, and the universe would make sure I got them. I counted on that.

After a two-year court battle, we ended up in a shared parenting agreement with a fifty-fifty split in time between both households. The caveat was he would not let go of the original temporary order for me to pay child support, so I had to continue to pay him. In my emotional state of unworthiness, I readily agreed, as my focus was primarily on getting to maintain an integral role in my children's lives. I got that. The money meant nothing. I could always make more of it.

Simultaneously, I was angry and bitter for a long time over having to pay him. We made the same salary. I felt like the only woman who had to pay child support in the entire world. I had never heard of that happening, and neither had anyone else that knew I paid. I know I wasn't alone in paying as the mother, but it sure seemed like it to me at the time.

In hindsight, it makes sense; when women desire liberation, with liberation comes accountability. I left him. I pay. When the man leaves the woman, he pays. It's the same thing, only this was 1997, and I was a forerunner on the issue, so I felt isolated and singled out. It's funny how perspective changes everything.

Nevertheless, everyone was shocked at how rare it was for a mother to be paying the father child support when both spouses worked. It was a progressive idea that had yet to catch on. This further fed into my low self-esteem, thus causing me to drink more. I felt like I wasn't good enough. In my mind, God was punishing me; that was why it turned out this way. I was in victim mode, and I was angry.

Not long after my divorce, I was able to quit drinking. It took me about fifteen months after the divorce was final to put alcohol down and never pick it back up to this day, not even a sip. My sobriety date is 1-1-01. How's that for new beginnings for all you numerology buffs out there!

I learned how to play the game early on in my law enforcement career simply by paying attention to my surroundings and emulating those I had respect for and who themselves had figured out the formula for success and advancement.

Lucky for me, I scored the highest on the promotional exam for sergeant and ended up being number one on the eligibility list. I purposely stayed at this rank for twelve years, as it afforded me the ability to remain in an assignment on dayshift with weekends and holidays off so I could spend time with my children. Many of my colleagues took every promotional exam that became available in order to advance as quickly as possible.

My mother died in January 2006. I soon felt myself being attracted to my best friend of ten years, Jean. I had met her in 1996 when I was promoted to sergeant and transferred to her area. She and I were more closely matched in every way. She had previously broken up with her long-term girlfriend, and I left the woman I was with.

The purpose of that relationship had run its course, and it was no longer deniable. Jean and I became life partners in mid-2006 and got married on June 26, 2015 or the day gay marriage became legal in the United States of America.

Going back to my career, in the end of 2007, I was transferred to Internal Affairs (IA) and was the first female in the history of the agency to be permanently assigned to IA. Internal Affairs was considered the police within the police, if you will. The division investigated alleged misconduct of officers. Having quit drinking at the midway point during the twelve total years I held the rank of sergeant, I believe, helped put me in a position to be transferred to IA. I had gained more credibility by no longer drinking with my subordinates.

Shortly thereafter, a lieutenant's exam was offered. I was privately asked to take the exam. I ended up being number one on that list of eligibility as well. A colleague who held the temporary rank of lieutenant and was currently assigned to IA with me had also taken the exam and was subsequently transferred out.

I was promoted to lieutenant in place, which was a rarity for the agency I worked in due to union issues. This meant I stayed assigned to Internal Affairs.

There's that hero syndrome again with the requisite resentment from others. I wasn't treated terribly though, because everyone knew it was ultimately the *big boss's* decision, and no one wanted to outwardly buck his authority. I still would have liked to have been a fly on the wall around the water cooler.

It's funny. I have a semblance of confidence in writing a book, in hindsight, because the big boss always said I could write. No one had ever said that to me prior to him. In fact, I felt the complete opposite about my abilities. When he said it to me, it made me proud of myself. It felt amazing. I could feel myself growing into my truth. I worked hard for it, and it felt good to be recognized for all my years of being honest, striving to be good at what I do, and doing the right thing.

I remained in IA for a total of three and a half years, and by the time it came to being promoted in my career to major, which happened to be a fiduciary appointment, I can humbly state that I had earned a reputation of being fair, honest, and smart.

It's interesting to me how I can say flattering things about myself now without feeling like I'm bragging. I used to self-deprecate to the point of ridiculousness, never saying anything remotely positive about myself or my abilities and then wondering why some people didn't treat me with the respect I felt I deserved.

I'm starting to get it. People will treat you the way you train or teach them to.

I had the fortunate experience in my career to work in various different divisions within the agency, enabling me to grow with each new assignment.

Likewise, I had a lot of painful experiences that augmented my growth. However, I want to say that tough people and tough circumstances are our greatest teachers. Be grateful for those moments, for they were designed to bring you closer to your true divine essence by showing you that which you are not! One has to be shown that which they *are not* in order to know who they *are*.

I retired in July 2012, and it didn't take me long to figure out that the ego that served me so well while working in law enforcement, to the point of permitting me to advance up the ladder of supervision as a female in a male-dominated workplace, was no longer serving me, and I needed to make some big changes.

It was becoming obvious I had a lot of work to do.

Sobriety and the Awakening

*Softness is not weakness. It takes courage to
stay delicate in a world so cruel."*
~Beau Taplin-Shed your sharp edges

You cannot be the greatest version of you while holding onto that which no longer serves you. Once you stop doing that thing you do to sabotage yourself and start listening for the guidance, the signs will come. They were always there. You weren't always listening.

Living contra to who I was, as a child growing up in my family and then carrying that on in my career in law enforcement, coupled with drinking myself to oblivion for over two decades of my life, was very hard on me physically, emotionally, psychologically, and spiritually.

My God, it was exhausting!

Speaking of God, I started turning to Him immediately upon putting the drink down. I mean, it was just the natural progression. I was beginning to again feel an unseen presence in and around me. One cannot cavort with the Almighty and be a practicing alcoholic. The two are mutually exclusive, diametrically opposed ways of being, thinking, and living. You cannot cover up or mute your true nature on a regular basis and be close to the Creator or Source. It just doesn't work that way.

Many parents were taught and therefore believed their children weren't capable of making decisions for themselves. It's people who are raised this way that pass that on to their own children. These parents feel they are the wisdom holders of the family and it is their job to impart all of it to their children. It is old-school thinking to believe the parents are the teachers of the children. In actuality, it is the children who come through the parents to be their teachers. Our children are our greatest teachers.

When one is raised in a hypercritical atmosphere, as in many of the generations of past, all too focused on expectations, perfection, and the projection of false outward appearances, one becomes too willing to believe they are not good enough and thus worthless when they fall short. If I did well or did nothing wrong, there was praise. However, I never wanted to make a mistake or not do well because the conditions became difficult. Disappointment, punishment, and yelling were the result, and my sensitivities couldn't handle it. I was a very sensitive child but learned to quickly cover it up in order to survive. In truth I have always loved deeply and been hurt easily.

When you know you are not perfect and must pretend that you are, a little piece of your worth or self-esteem dies because you know you're living a lie. You are a walking, talking, living personification of falsehoods. I had fear but never felt allowed to express it. I wanted to shout, "Hey, I'm really scared here," but I had never heard that in my life and knew I wasn't allowed to say it. No one was allowed to say they were scared. We were all scared but no more so than anyone else.

What I now know is no one is confident at all times. If such a person exists, rest assured, he is not well liked. Push on through your fear, doubt, and skepticism, and you'll inspire those around you to be brave.

When childhood fear is rejected, shame becomes your cloak. Oftentimes there's a huge disconnect with the internal reality people are experiencing and the outward projection they are giving.

When you're raised with this idea that we are perfect and must project that nothing—that is, no-thing—is wrong, there is no outlet for emotion. The unexpressed emotion builds energetically in the body. I'm afraid and don't feel perfect; therefore, there is something wrong with me. So, many people who cover up their true emotions and have no outlet for them turn to alcohol or drugs. Alcohol is a natural anesthetic; it anesthetizes the emotional and physical bodies. When this happens, it makes it much easier to not face yourself and the truth that you're being unauthentic.

Whenever real emotion bubbles to the surface and you quash it with alcohol, it pushes it down into the physical body where it lays in wait for disease to begin to take hold. That is what disease is ... dis-ease, ill at ease or not at ease. That is what alcohol does; it is one of a myriad ways we humans mask fear and run from emotion.

Here's a newsflash: we all have fear! It's scary down here. But if we could just acknowledge it and say to one another or to our children, "I know you're scared, so am I, but we are going to do 'it' anyway," the relief and thus empowerment that would result would astonish you. Maybe then we could all flourish emotionally and be physically healthy. Unfortunately, many of us are instead taught to cover or mask it with bravado. The better you are at masking your pain and fear, the more touted you are in society, it seems. According to Teal Swan, cancer is childhood trauma and unresolved childhood grief. It's the body's wake-up call to the soul. It's in essence saying, "Hey, you need to look at this." You've got to address your stuck childhood trauma once and for all.

Repressed emotion eventually turns into physical illness. When dis-ease or lack of ease finally manifests itself, you can bet you are a longtime sufferer of your own misaligned thoughts, albeit mostly not your own original thoughts but those you inherited, learned, or were passed down generationally to you.

Misaligned thoughts? What thoughts? Misaligned from what or whom? They are the thoughts that you aren't enough—tall enough, short enough, smart enough, athletic enough, pretty enough, thin enough, rich enough, nice enough, light enough, dark enough, talented enough, good enough, or any other thought stemming from a place of lack.

When your thoughts are from a place of lack, you're misaligned from your true nature, every time, in every circumstance. The reality is you're a piece of Source energy, a spark of the divine, and already perfect just as you are. So is everybody else.

The old way of thinking where one is born with no idea of who they are and it takes the parents, teachers, and entire community to mold the child into someone that fits into society is dying.

We are awakening to the idea that each soul who comes to earth to experience for the divine comes so with an already intact blueprint for their individual, specific purpose, and it's the job of the parents, grandparents, caregivers, teachers, and society at large to coax and facilitate that growth of coming into one's own by loving, supporting, and gently guiding the young being on the journey of their choice, without judgment or attempts to sway the child into a direction that is not of his or her own choosing.

As you are shifting into an enlightened individual, you will begin to realize that you are not the same person you used to be. The things you used to tolerate have become intolerable. Where you once remained quiet, you are now speaking your truth. Where you once battled and argued, you are now choosing to remain silent. You now realize it's more important to keep the peace than to be right. You are beginning to understand the value of your voice. There are oftentimes situations and sometimes people that you no longer should give your time, energy, and focus to. It's a good reminder to prepare for many changes you will see along your journey to enlightenment.

It always amazes me how much better my life became once I put down the alcohol. My life had truly become unmanageable, and I was no longer even able to hear the whispers of Spirit trying to capture my attention. I had been so used to turning away and doing what I wanted to do without any regard for who I was hurting or how much damage I was inflicting upon myself that when the fog cleared from the drinking, I felt reborn.

I never knew why turning to God, Spirit, Source, the Creator was referred to as "born again" until I personally experienced it. I became a new me.

When you've been turning away from the spiritual path you were meant to be on for years and then you find the entrance to it, it truly does feel nothing short of being reborn. Spirituality begins to blossom into healing. One is compelled into searching for a better way of life, a more peaceful existence, one that is fulfilling and maybe even, God forbid ... happy!

There's an Alcoholics Anonymous (AA) saying that the first year after quitting drinking or sobriety, you're in the "pink cloud." You're walking on air, your sense of smell returns, and all of your senses are supercharged, enhanced, and operating at what seems like somewhere between maximum capacity and euphoria. It feels very similar to youth and experiencing things for the first time.

It's also true that an alcoholic emotionally ceases growing the moment they pick up their first drink. So, here I was at thirty-six years old operating at the level of a petulant thirteen-year-old. Nice, real, real nice. And by that, I mean not so much! I had a lot of work to do.

Once one surrenders to that Achilles' heel that is preventing their growth, whatever it may be, growth can begin. Not only does everyone have an Achilles' heel, I promise you know what yours is, even if subconsciously, and therefore how to heal it.

First, you must admit you have it, surrender to it, and then let it go. Give it back to the universe to transmute into pure, positive energy and love.

Love is really all there is. It cannot be realized if you're continuously mired in playing around with your dark side.

Waiting for a Sign: Happiness and Fear

Every death is a joyful birth into a
higher dimension of being.
—James Van Praagh

I knew what I needed to do but was petrified to do it. I knew enough about what I had read to know working on your psyche or inner self was very difficult and painful. Hence, most people don't try too hard to delve in and confront it.

The period of time when you search for your inner being can be referred to as the dark night of the soul. It sounds ominous and creepy.

The ego is on constant guard to protect you from the real you or your authentic self and essence. The ego is well aware of how powerful the soul is and therefore has an invested interest in seeing that all of its earthly needs get met. It's directly correlated to the primal urge to survive. The soul is not fed by the ego or its desire for rank and judgment.

When one begins to ascend, the ego becomes terrified of annihilation or extinction, as it instinctively knows that a conscious being that is fully aware of who s/he is rarely lives from the ego. The ego lies.

Now, if you're like me, you're thinking, *How in the world am I going to get rid of my ego?* It's firmly in place, and it's what I always relied on to get me through the tough times when I felt attacked or threatened. Especially in my law enforcement career, my ego served me enormously.

The ego's job is to protect a person from attack. It is tied directly into living your physical existence by successfully navigating the earth world and keeping you from literal death. It's the primal you. It's that section of the person that exists exclusively when you're on earth having a human experience.

Therefore, no one ought to get rid of the ego. You can't. It serves an essential purpose throughout life. However, I've learned that in order to live a more spiritual and thus conscious life, I must live from my heart and not so much my mind, which is so strongly connected to the ego.

This section of the book is about my fear of getting to know myself completely and the doubt that I would be able to successfully do it. I had started believing in a greater force than myself when I quit drinking about a decade prior, but I hadn't really delved any deeper than that. What was I hiding from myself?

We lie to ourselves the very best.

As soon as I retired from my law enforcement career, I began to search for answers to the truth of why we are here. Why am I here, specifically? What is this thing called life all about? What is my specific purpose? Where is happiness? How do you find it?

When I was working, I always said I couldn't wait to retire because I just knew that then I would be happy.

I have done that projection of future happiness all throughout my life, always looking to the next best *future* idea, condition, event, benchmark, situation, circumstance, or anything other than where I currently was in each of those moments. I had it all backwards. "I'll be happy when ..." instead of "I'm happy now because of ..."

It went a little like this: *I'll be happy once I get into middle school because primary school is for babies.* I got to middle school. Then it was *I'll be happy when I get to high school.* High school came and went ... still searching. Then I said I'd be happy once I graduated college (and have been wishing to go back ever since), but with graduating came the daunting realization, *I now must become gainfully employed in order to support myself for the rest of my life.*

That was a reality check.

The next big event would surely be the answer: getting married, having a baby, having another baby, wishing them the ability to sit up, crawl, walk, and then back to infancy again, getting divorced, getting promoted at work, again and again and again, finally being recognized for the honesty and integrity I brought to a career that is typically dominated by ego-driven men, retirement, then grandchildren. It's always just one more event away—then happiness will no longer elude.

Still, not a lot of happy in my life! Ugh! Obviously, future projection of happiness does not work and is *not* the answer to happiness.

I could go on and on and on about the next "thing" that was coming that was surely going to be "it." All of it brought periods of happiness, fleeting moments of bliss, but it never stayed around for very long. I'm not even convinced that happiness works like that, a final destination.

Rather, I believe happiness comes in little pieces, periodically peppering the mundane. It's that ever-elusive emotion that keeps us striving for more of it.

People try too hard to be happy. Happiness rests in the present now moment. We put so much emphasis on and pressure to attain it that when it shows up during a nice early morning walk at dawn, we often don't even recognize it because we've pumped up our expectations so high it eludes us in the moment it appears.

Happiness is not a state of being but more of an experience or collection of experiences. We have many experiences of happiness throughout our lives. Maybe we need to start defining happiness as fleeting moments rather than a vague state of constant consciousness as a successful benchmark of attainment. I'm sure many more people would realize they are already truly happy and have been all along.

It's like anything else that you have too much of; you grow tired and bored with it. You barely recognize it anymore once something becomes a constant. Just as no one would want to stay in perpetual anger or fear or indifference, perpetual happiness would get old too. There would be no appreciation for it. Maybe being happy is as simple as the absence of sorrow and pain.

I believe that is the precise reason we all came to earth in the first place. Staying in a space of unconditional love 24/7, such as in the spirit realm, is so sublime it dictates a desire to experience its opposite, if for no other reason than to once again be able to truly appreciate it upon our return home from our earthly sojourn.

Boredom is a condition of the soul regardless of where that soul resides, either on earth during an incarnation or on the other side (heaven, Spirit, home, etc.).

But I digress.

This is how I write … all over the map in shotgun form. It's pretty much why I chose to self-publish, as I don't think any reputable publishing company would particularly appreciate my style. I kind of just wing it. I have all these thoughts, and I write them as I feel them, and then when I go to put them together in some kind of cohesive fashion, it becomes very hard to build a bridge and make it flow from one thought form to the next.

So, you end up having a hodgepodge of thoughts that somewhat interconnect to build a story of how I came to understand the universe and its purpose from the limited and finite perspective of one sliver or spark of the infinite Being or Source, which is me.

We are all individual sparks of the divine or source energy having a physical experience.

So this chapter is about waiting for signs and being afraid of them and what they will say. What if I don't want to listen to the suggestion? What if it disrupts the direction of my own intention?

It isn't like that at all and isn't scary in actuality once you begin to sincerely look for the signs of your personal predetermined direction. It actually simplifies life.

It's funny when synchronicities line up in life that let you know you're on the right track. Or let you know you're in "the vortex," like Abraham-Hicks would say. As I began to write this book, I would have successful days of writing, and other days were just heavy with the weight of the self-perceived burden of having committed to the universe or God, if you will, to write a book about my life and how I became a spiritual being.

Anyway, during the initial writing phase of this book, I got up in the morning a little later that normal (okay, a lot later) because it was, after all, February in Ohio, so that needs no more explanation for anyone who's been to the Midwest in February. Life becomes perpetually dreary, ad nauseam.

Feeling the weight of the daunting task, I grabbed my coffee and my tablet and opened my e-mail in hopes of gaining my daily literary pick-me-up from Mike Dooley via his *TUT—A Note from the Universe*™, and this is what it said:

Funny, Stephanie, most folks "there" are waiting for a sign of sorts from folks "here", before they make a move, take action, or commit.

Same "here"!

Let this be your sign,

The Universe

Wow! Really? I am always amazed and a little giddy each and every time life shows me a sign that I know came from nowhere other than "above" or "there." It actually was the impetus to begin writing the book.

In that moment, I realized since retirement I had been waiting for Spirit to tell me what to do next. I was learning that isn't how it works. You have to go first, and then when the action is in alignment with your purpose, the universe lines up behind you in support. It's one great way to determine if you're doing what you're supposed to be doing. Is life smooth or extraordinarily bumpy? Life will have occasional bumps, but I'm talking about one bad situation after another as if someone or something is trying desperately to get your attention. Listen.

So, thank you, universe, Source, All that Is, for the little nudge to spur me into action instead of me sitting around waiting for the action to come to me.

I remember a time when reading those words would've sent me into a tailspin from the self-induced pressure so hard that I wouldn't recover for months if not years. You can sign up for your own personalized ditties from the universe at www.TUT.com.

I think I'm getting this waiting-for-a-sign thing down. It seems fairly easy and not nearly as scary as I thought it was prior to actually looking for it. Yay! You see, it's all about perspective. What do you hear when you read that sentence? "Most folks 'there' are waiting for a sign of sorts from folks 'here,' before they make a move, take action or commit."

For me, I used to hear a caveat to the sentence and infer that I can't take a step, make a move, take action, or commit unless and until I had it all figured out to the nth degree of perfection, all the way to the end. I had to know the outcome prior to the commencement, or I was reluctant to engage. I had to know I would be successful or I wouldn't try. I still wrestle with this from time to time.

In reality, it kept me spiritually stuck, never moving forward with the gifts locked inside of me, afraid of not being perfect or good enough.

I read into the message of taking a step as the equivalent of having to build a castle or mansion of such enormous size, magnitude, and proportion that I would invariably overwhelm myself and convince myself that I didn't have what it takes to move forward and make my mark in the world.

In reality, I have already made my mark, and so have you, just by being born and living life every day, by taking little baby steps along the way. For most of my fifty-two years on earth, I've heard it said that just existing here on earth was enough. I never believed it ... until now. Now I realize I am an anchor of love and light.

Now I would like to share some experiences early on in my spiritual awakening of some signs my deceased mother gave me, starting at the precise moment of her death in 2006 and ramping up in the year of my retirement in mid-2012.

I had been reading many books about the afterlife, life between lives, and reincarnation in a desperate attempt to make contact with her and know definitively in my heart and soul that we do go on after death and she wasn't gone forever.

My mother's death was the impetus to spiritual growth for me. All four of my siblings (my eldest stepbrother had died from alcohol-related issues at thirty-three) were at our parents' home in Florida at the end of Mom's life. She was able to be home due to the wonderful organization of Hospice. Immediately upon her death or crossing over, the song "Best Thing That Ever Happened to Me" by Gladys Knight and The Pips (1973) came on the radio. My sister and I were dressing her in the gown our dad had picked out for her to be cremated in. This is extremely significant, as it was my parents' favorite song. The entire family had previously planned her funeral service, prior to her death, in the family room where she lay in the Hospice hospital bed, seemingly in a comatose state. We were discussing what songs to play at her service. That song was given paramount importance as we all discussed it.

Furthermore, the radio had been playing for five straight days, at the suggestion of the Hospice nurse, as it is believed to have a calm and soothing effect on the dying. The radio station was never changed; we had continuously played her favorite station that played oldies from the seventies. It was her favorite, I suspect, because that was the time in her life when she met my stepfather, who was the love of her life.

Anyway, that song never played during those five days and nights. I was there the entire time and heard the loop of same songs the station commonly played at certain times of the day.

Yet her favorite song, "Best Thing That Ever Happened to Me," came on the radio within minutes of her passing. In fact, I was so overwrought with grief I didn't even notice. It was my sister who looked up at me and said, "Listen to the song!"

I couldn't believe it. I impulsively yelled out to my entire family, "Listen to the song! Mom played her song for us!" It was a life-changing moment for me. It was then I knew. I could *feel* it. The spirit is eternal. My mother's death triggered my awakening.

After that, my mother began to communicate with me via electricity rather regularly. At the time of her death, I had yet to hear about departed souls communicating via electricity and lighting. I now know it is a fairly common method, as we are all energy of differing forms and various vibrations.

When I returned home to Ohio from Florida, I immediately noticed two of my three garage lights were out. I had just changed them. This was weird. Then, upon stepping inside, I noticed the ambient light that we leave on when we are away was not on. I checked, and it had burned out. It no longer worked. I immediately turned another light on in order to be able to see, and it "popped" off the moment I turned it on.

What was going on?

Throughout the next couple of days, I came to find approximately seven to nine lights burned out. These were lights in special places used for ambient lighting, just like my mom loved to use in her own home. It was a veritable smorgasbord of activity that my mother, along with the universe, was using to awaken me. It had to be in order to capture my attention. I was a tough nut to crack.

It was undeniable. It worked!

The following is a list of a few ways my mother has used since crossing over (transitioning) to communicate with us, whether it's just to say hello or point us in the right direction:

- Playing a song at a particular poignant moment.

- Turning off or on lights.

- Pennies left in spots I find on special occasions or when I'm thinking heavily about her. One time when I started a part-time job after being retired for two years, my mother left literally twenty-five new pennies in the parking lot I was sweeping. They shined so brightly they blinded me.

- On my first birthday after her crossing, a turtle came into my fenced-in yard all the way from a faraway pond, and it had never happened before.

- On the night prior to my last day of work, I was looking for my coat badge so I could turn it in. I knew I hadn't taken it off my coat, but it was no longer there. I looked everywhere, including my junk drawer several times. I went to bed upset, as I had never lost any of my law enforcement equipment and was devastated to have to end my long career on that note. It's a big deal when a badge, ID, or gun is lost, and several reports must be made. I got up the next morning and decided to look in my junk drawer again, and lo and behold there it was. Now I know for certain it wasn't there when I looked seventeen times the day before while taking everything out of it. However, I believe it was my mother's energy that manifested it in the drawer for me. She knew how embarrassed I would have been to report my duty badge was missing on the day I retired.

- She turns the family room ceiling fanlight on during conversations about her or at precise moments for impact. In June 2013, my wife, Jean, and I were discussing the possibility of opening a business. My cell phone rang with the caller ID saying "Unknown," which was extremely rare at that time. I said hello, and the familiar prerecorded lady's voice said good-bye. I had been reading Allison DuBois's book *We Are Their Heaven* the night before and read how many spirits communicate with their loved ones on earth by calling their phone, and then no one is there. I had thought to myself at the time, *My mother never does that one!* Then, lo and behold, she did it the following day during a potentially life-changing conversation my wife and I were having. She had been gone for seven years.

- My mother hadn't turned the light on for a while when on the first day of my brother's job, who was living with us at the time, she turned it on and freaked him out!

- At one point around 2013, I was at the doctor with my biological father, who divorced my mother some forty years prior, and I was reading a book on how souls who cross over communicate with those of us who are still living. He asked me what I was reading, and I told him about the book, and he scoffed, as I knew he would. He is not one to believe in the intangible, and I'm gilding that lightly. Anyway, as I was telling him my mother oftentimes still communicates with me from the other side through electricity, the entire office's lights and power went out for about twenty seconds, which was long enough for the entire staff to go into a mild panic, musing aloud at how this had never happened before and worrying how it could potentially negatively impact their equipment. When the lights came back on, I was looking at my Dad, and he said, "Kind of like that?" in a joking manner yet visibly shaken and in awe. I said, "Yes, just like that." Thanks, Mom.

- My second birthday after retirement, 2013, I prayed for my mother to turn the light on in order to wish me a happy birthday. I was becoming awake and was doing a lot of work on myself. No light came on that day, to my dismay. I had a discussion with my then partner, now wife, about why my mother wouldn't oblige me on my birthday, and she said she didn't think spirit worked that way. "They aren't on any time schedule, and they don't respond to demands. Rather, they send signs when they want to, not necessarily when we want them to," she said. I accepted that as truth. The very next morning, the day after my birthday, two robin bird babies fledged from a nest close to our house, and one of them bounced on foot all the way over to me, standing deep inside my garage, and stopped right at my feet, looking up at me. I bent down (in tears) to pick him or her up, and it flittered away under the car and then out of the garage. I knew it was sent by my mom because robins were her sign, which she sent me the spring following her passing. They would peck on my windows and land right near me all the time. It's funny because I had expected it to be cardinals, as they are the most common bird sent from spirit to communicate with the living. Leave it to my mom to be different! It wasn't until my wife, Jean, told me the story of why a robin's breast is red that I understood the reason why my mother sent them instead of cardinals. Fable says the robin's breast is red due to it touching the brow of Jesus as he was bleeding from the crown of thorns as he hung on the cross. This signified to me she made it home, as she had said just two weeks prior to her death that she had wished she had "believed" and envied those that did.

I had been worried she may not have made it to heaven due to her nonbelief in God. I was not convinced at that point that going to church was not a prerequisite in order to make it to Heaven. Mom wasn't sure there was a God (I guess; we never really talked about it) and hadn't gone to church for the last half of her life. Yet here was her soul freely communicating with me from the other side. The idea was freeing to me, as I had never really gone to church except as a little child from birth to seven and for about a two-year period just before and after my mom passed.

The church teaches it is the only way to God. Therefore, I thought one had to attend church in order to be accepted into heaven, yet that idea never felt good to me. I always felt a pang in my gut when I would guilt myself about not going to church—not about my absence from church but that I didn't feel like going and thought I should. It was as if it was wisdom I had known all along yet was so contra to what I had heard all my life from others who had regularly attended church. A light of truth was ignited within me. It was a sense of knowing. I was learning God was everywhere, not just in church.

I don't know what I expected in terms of signs and being able to read them, but in reality, it was easy, and the unwavering feeling that it was definitively coming from my mother in spirit was undeniable.

Once you begin to pay attention to the signs, they appear everywhere and become easier to read. They were always there; I just couldn't read them, as I had no frame of reference and had never been taught how.

Our spirit guides often send us signs, as do our departed loved ones.

I was waking up.

Shadow Work

If you want to awaken all of humanity, then awaken
all of yourself, if you want to eliminate the suffering
in the world, then eliminate all that is dark and
negative in yourself. Truly, the greatest gift you have
to give is that of your own self-transformation.
—Lao Tzu

There is a term in the spiritual arena called the "shadow
self." This self, in Jungian psychology, is called the
"shadow" or "shadow aspect" and refers to the unconscious
aspect of the personality that the conscious ego does not
identify in itself.

Anytime you speak to any spiritually enlightened
individual, he or she will say you must do your shadow
work in order to rid yourself of what is holding you back
from going to the next level of enlightenment.

Generally, people do not like to face their darker, more
negative aspects. Because one tends to reject or remain
ignorant of the least desirable aspects of one's personality,
the shadow is largely negative, of which a person is not
fully conscious.

The shadow self definition according to Carl Jung is: "the unconscious or unaware part of the personality that tends to be largely negative, instinctive and irrational and prone to projection."

Projection is a theory in psychology in which humans defend themselves against their unpleasant impulses by denying their existence while attributing them to others. For example, a habitually rude person may continuously accuse other people of being rude.

It, in essence, is the practice of putting undesirable feelings or emotions onto someone else rather than admitting to having them ourselves. Everyone does it. However, the more conscious you are of it, the better chance you have of catching and thus correcting yourself.

A good way to catch yourself projecting is to become aware of when you have strong negative feelings about someone and then ask yourself why you are reacting that way. Then go deeper and ask if there is anything about their bothersome behavior you can see within yourself.

At first you'll find yourself rebuking the idea of you having any traits similar to the ones you abhor in others. But like anything else, as soon as you do it enough, you will see the truth of how you have been defending your shadow self through projection. In time, it will become painfully obvious when you project.

There are positive aspects hidden in the shadow, especially in people with low self-esteem, which is a category I fell squarely into. Carl Jung said everyone carries a shadow, and the less it is identified in the conscious life of the individual, the blacker and denser it is. It may be partly linked to more primitive animal instincts, which are superseded during early childhood by the conscious mind.

So it makes sense to lighten and dilute the shadow if you want to lead a happier, more conscious life. It allows you to stop being pissed off at everyone for everything!

Shadow work is often touted as being a necessity in order to continue on the spiritual journey of self-actualization, enlightenment, ascension, or whatever term you would like to use that depicts the soul growth in order to live a more conscious life.

When I say conscious life, I'm referring to Christ consciousness. I'm referring to being more unconditionally loving, nonjudgmental, and compassionate.

So, what exactly is involved with shadow work? Shadow work is essentially delving into that side of us we do not like. The parts of us we keep hidden from others or in the shadows. We all have a shadow side, and it takes great guts and courage to face it.

The good news is having a darker side or aspect to your personality provides great foundation for and has been linked to creativity. So, find out what your shadow self is all about and embrace it. By doing this, you will be integrating your darker aspects with your conscious mind and making whole your soul in the interim.

As stated before, the road to leading a happy life begins with healing the self at the soul level.

There is a great tool I used to assist me in facing my shadow self, a book by Debbie Ford called *The Dark Side of the Light Chasers*. It was a step-by-step process of just how to do this shadow work. I will be very transparent and share with you what came up for me by taking you along the journey.

The first exercise requires a large block of uninterrupted time and consists of sitting in quiet meditation and asking yourself many scripted questions. After a short time, you are to write down what you come up with, without thinking about it too hard. Just put pen to paper and see what comes up without filtering and or judging it. Freestyle.

The first question is, *what are you most afraid of by looking inward and doing this shadow work?*

Here is what came up for me:

I am most afraid of self-revelation. I am frightened to expose my most inner self, the one who is so soft and gel like it morphs into whoever is in my proximity in order to fit in with blatant disregard for who I am. I am the light, the way, and I bury it deeply within in order to not be shunned by others and not feel loved by them. My biggest fear is to be unloved. I am terrified to be left alone, unloved, and disconnected to Source. I'm unaware of my own ability to connect to Him on my own. I'm going through the learning process of just how to do that now at this moment and point in time.

Now, *what aspects of your life need transforming?*

I must transform my ability to make more people happy by being myself, beautiful self. Not to be assumptive that I have to make them happy by telling them all what to do, how, when, where, etc. ... I must transform my thinking from being outside everyone to being within all people. Be the change I want to see in others. Don't preach. Do. Be. Just as in heaven the ones who will resonate with your vibration will stay, those not ready will go. Not an issue as we are all one anyway and you'll see them again soon enough. Then when you do, you will understand why it was. Transform your perception of enlightenment to more of an everyday existence from a lofty out-of-this world perception of how to be tomorrow. To be enlightened truly is to live every ordinary day like it was your only chance to experience the earth world ... with gratitude and hopeless love, and then gifts will be bestowed upon thee.

Okay. Wow! I'm not sure where that came from, but I know it wasn't just me and my conscious mind. I get it—the idea is to let go enough to push your conscious ego aside and delve deep. I have found when you let go and really listen to your heart, you will find that spark of the divine that resides in us all.

The next exercise is to ask yourself in the same meditative fashion *what you want to accomplish* by reading the book. For this I said:

I want to clear all the blocks in my chakras and energy centers that disallow my ability to become an ascended being, and I want to confront the dark aspects of myself, meet them, greet them, welcome them so they can no longer rule me and prevent me from my highest and best potential being. I want to clear my energy and rid myself of all the dark/negative energy that keeps interrupting my development. I want to accomplish the last part of my journey of detoxifying my spirit of earthly garbage that I put in place for protection of my vulnerable, divine, sweet, and loving essence. Stop covering up my sweet and tender side and merge my dark within the light in order to go forth in total light and stop running from myself of old. Accept in totality and forgive myself for living contra to my true, pure essence in order to learn my lessons in preparation for this aspect of my journey.

Now, ask yourself, *what are you most afraid someone else will find out about you?* I said:

I am most afraid someone will find out I am a loving spirit who isn't tough at all. I'm just a small creature in a huge, living, breathing universe that wants desperately to be loved and fit in. That I care way too much what other people think of me. That I worry too much about the physical world and all its shiny objects, and I want to change but don't know how. That I need help from others and I may not always have the answer to what they question.

Then ask yourself, *what are you most afraid of finding out about yourself?* I said:

I am most afraid of finding out that I am not that special. That I'm just like everyone else, not a cut above. I want to be special to God and everyone in the world. I'm afraid to find out I'm no one special in particular. I'm afraid to find out I don't matter. I'm nothing. I'm no better than the average. I'm not good enough for any of this work. That the divine Lord God will not want to use me in his service of love to all that is. That he's un-chosen me. I'll make him mad that it's taking me so long to get here.

Now, *what is the biggest lie you've told yourself?* For me it was:

I don't matter. I am never enough. I'm no one's anything. I'm not special or worthy of great things.

Then, *what is the biggest lie you've ever told someone else?*

They weren't good enough or able to be whatever they wanted or needed to be. That the limits of the earth were insurmountable.

And finally, *what is the thing most able to stop you from doing the necessary work to transform your life?*

That all my loved ones would not support me and think I'm leaving them and am weird or crazy and no longer have time for them in my life. Everyone leaving me because I'm not the person I was, they remember, or who they want me to be any longer. To be alone.

Another exercise in Debbie Ford's book, *The Dark Side of the Light Chasers,* is to ask yourself and write down *what you need to do in order to let go of any old emotional toxicity you have been carrying around.* I wrote:

You must get out of your head and into your heart more. Don't believe others who try and bring you down because they do not understand who you are and where you're going. They are not walking your path. You are. You can release your stored emotional toxicity by forgiving all those that have hurt you, whether intentionally or unintentionally, and know in your soul they all love you and are doing exactly what you asked of them in order to bring you to this point of self-introspection. Keep meditating and getting in touch with me, your sacred self, in order to remember who you are and why you're here on earth at this time. Your journey is special; don't expect everyone or even anyone to understand it, for it's your journey and yours alone. The assistance you receive is preordained just as the resistance is. The resistance is to spur you on to go forth and keep seeking the answers to your individual truth.

Meeting my shadow, *the first word to come up was ...*

Ashamed! I am so ashamed it has taken me this long to remember my purpose out of turning away from my sacred self. I've always felt I was no good, not worthy of God's love due to how contra I was living. I've never felt like He would want to bestow gifts upon me because I trounced around in the muck of life and didn't lift myself up to Him. I'm a bad girl. I'm stupid. I'm too gullible and naïve and dumb and couldn't survive on my own to be trusted to make my own decisions for myself because I'm too stupid to make the right ones. I'm too emotional, too impatient, too selfish, too indulgent, and basically unable to be mature enough to stand on my own two feet and raise a family in a healthy and vibrant manner. I was never told by my parents that they had faith in me to be successful on my own. I'm either not thin enough, smart enough, or cunning enough to succeed in life. I better get a man to assist me no matter how he treats me. Yet not many men would want me because I'm too masculine, I swear too much, I like hanging with the men, and am not thin enough. Better settle for what you can get when you first are offered to be loved forever. You are a "bitch in heat." What the hell's the matter with you? People aren't going to listen to you when you are looking and acting the way you do. Just get it together and make the appearances like all is perfect. Nothing wrong behind these doors! We're good. Not really.

These were the unconscious tapes running in the recesses of my mind sabotaging my self-acceptance and, thus, spiritual advancement. I had heard all of these statements at some point in my life if not several times. I had learned to believe them and to believe myself unworthy.

The next part of the exercise is to *envision your sacred self embracing your shadow self and realizing full integration.*

I envisioned my sacred self as a small child of seven years old who met the dark side of me at seven years old as well. The sacred self kept denying the dark side's attempts to dance with him. The dark side was black in color and male. The sacred self was white in color and female. The two began to hold one hand of each other and in a slow and reticent way began to teasingly dance with one another. As the dance went on and the two became more aligned with one another, they began spinning and spinning, melding their two essences together into a whole. The color meshed and grew lighter and lighter until once again it was white. The children also grew up as they were entwined in the dance of spinning. As they spun faster and faster, becoming one being, they cast off of themselves dark mist- like-material in huge waves of clustered old, dark, emotionally toxic material that was then absorbed or reintegrated into the atmosphere and dissipated into the white light of happiness and positivity and love! Once the dance ended, the sacred self stood before me as a fully integrated being of the light. The feeling of closure was there.

Incidentally, my dark side was a young child, androgynous in nature and stooped down, cowering in the corner when I met him/her. S/he was scared to death, alone and frightened of his/her shadow. Stuck in time in a purgatory-like existence. Hell.

After this exercise that took about three hours to complete, I felt a comprehensive sense of release. S/he (I) didn't want to exist by himself but was forced into existence out of fear and desperate desire to please his/her parents and elders. Now s/he has been released through integration into the whole of myself, ready to tackle the next phase of life.

Another exercise consisted of asking yourself, *what are the core beliefs that are running my life?* At the time I completed this exercise, this is what I wrote down:

A core belief of mine is that the world revolves around me. I'm the only one affected by life's ups and downs. If I'm hurting, that's the only thing that matters at the time. I'm never going to feel whole. Everyone lets me down. I'm going to continuously walk God's green earth half of a whole. No matter how much good I do for myself and others, I myself will never experience the happy fulfillment of wholeness.

And the reason is because I don't deserve it because I'm not good enough.

The next step is to identify where you adopted the belief, why you have it, and does the belief empower you.

I learned that the belief did empower me because if I didn't feel this way, I would always let others run me and my life. That had been a consistent problem up to recent history … letting others dictate what was best for me without figuring it out and choosing for myself.

I would have to give up impatience in order to alter this belief. I would have to be less self-centered and give up the spotlight in any dealings with others.

I would have to give up martyrdom.

Debbie Ford's next exercise is to *write a letter to your core beliefs thanking them for serving you.* The idea is to let go of these negative beliefs with gratitude, as they no longer serve you.

Here is my letter to all my core beliefs:

Thank you for serving me in my life and enabling me to finish early in a career where I needed to take care of myself or else I would become lost, physically ill, and not able to make it out intact, like so many others before me. I am inventing a new core belief to replace the one that the world revolves around me. The world is comprised of many parts that make up the whole of humanity. We all count and matter equally. Without one part, the whole is not truly whole. I am not alone.

We are all necessary and equal parts of the whole! No more. No less.

The next exercise was to *write down a word you cannot fully embrace or love:*

Selfish.

When I was growing up, my mother called me selfish in several instances when I felt like I was merely protecting myself from someone taking advantage of me or when I put myself before another in a situation where it felt necessary so as not to be taken advantage of or manipulated. I never intended to be selfish. It never seemed as if I was being selfish in and of itself—it was a protective maneuver from the manipulations of others that I so easily succumbed to. It made me feel like I should sacrifice myself for others even when it didn't feel right, and I had no desire to do so.

"I am not selfish. I am a loving, generous person who will not allow another to take advantage of me," was the statement I came up with to heal that shameful aspect of being viewed as selfish by the most important person in my life, my mother.

A good exercise to try as suggested in Debbie Ford's book is to *write down five to ten words that inspire you.* Mine were:

- charismatic
- dynamic
- spiritual
- elevated
- open
- all-encompassing
- teacher
- wise
- powerful

Now write a mission statement using your inspiring words. She suggested you make it powerful! So I did:

"I am a beautiful soul on my way to becoming a charismatic, dynamic, spiritually, wise teacher of others with a powerful message that will be open for anyone who wants an all-encompassing program in order to elevate one's soul."

There were many more exercises that have the potential to dredge up very dark aspects of the personality. I have not included all of them.

We subconsciously call forth that which is within us through people mirroring back to us those aspects we know we must acknowledge in order for healing to occur.

The miracle occurs when you truly own and embrace an undesirable aspect of yourself. At that point, the person that is serving as your mirror will either stop acting out the behavior or you will become able to choose not to have this person in your life.

The great news about this hard work is when you unplug, you no longer need another person to mirror your shadow back to you. Because you will be more whole yourself, you'll naturally gravitate to those who reflect your wholeness. If our soul's purpose is to become complete, we'll continually call forth what we need to see to be whole. As we own more of ourselves, healthier people will show up in our lives.

Remember ... if you zero in on an unlikeable aspect of someone else, it's because you possess that similar aspect within your shadow.

Some poignant and well-known spiritual philosophies that many have said are:

What we fear ... appears!

What you can't be with ... won't let you be!

What we resist ... persists!

When you own all the aspects or traits of the universe, good and bad, you'll understand that every aspect within you has something to teach you.

The *only* time it is *not* okay to express your emotion is when you're hurting another person (or yourself)! However, when you come face-to-face with a shadow aspect of yourself you detest, express it.

Scream as hard as you can. Scream therapy is an actual therapeutic modality. It is extremely cathartic. Use a plastic bat and a stack of pillows. Visualize bringing the bat up over our head and coming down as hard as you can on the resisted trait, owning it and whacking away. After releasing all the emotion, it becomes much easier to go to the mirror and own a trait.

If we embrace the negative trait internally, we no longer have to express or create it externally.

Then we can start to genuinely feel good about ourselves and begin to believe in ourselves. And then you can say ...

Stephanie Klumpp

I am enough!
You are enough!
And ...
Together we are enough exponentially!

Professional Readings

We teach best what we most need to learn.

—Richard Bach, *Illusions:*
The Adventures of a Reluctant Messiah

In the beginning, it didn't take me long to figure out I needed help getting started on my journey of spiritual ascension, enlightenment, or self-actualization. I needed some outside professional guidance and assistance. I was new to the new age spiritual scene and community, and I hadn't a clue as to where or how to begin working on myself.

My first thought was I must find out who I truly am. Who or what is my soul? Where has it been? Where is it going? I felt this would best identify myself to me. To me, it was logical to know my past in order to help me define who I was today.

I needed to reach out. I'm not good at that.

I was nearly fifty years old and felt a little like maybe it was too late to fix myself. I later learned there is no time that is inappropriate to awaken. The time is now. No time like the present. It's just important to actually do it.

Upon retirement, I started reading books. I read all kinds of spiritual books, dozens of them, in fact. I learned almost immediately that in order to embrace this thing called enlightenment, one must first believe in its very base tenet of reincarnation. In other words, a belief that the soul (spirit) is eternal, and along with the eternity of the soul, most believe it chooses to live lives on earth and by taking on a human form, sometimes thousands of times. I quickly learned we all come here with spirit guides who guide us along our journey, whether we are aware of it or not.

In its natural state, the essence of the soul/spirit is simply pure energy.

It all began by finding a local intuitive, by a neighbor's referral, who I consulted regularly, and he would occasionally, as intuitively guided, point me in the direction of specific practitioners. These practitioners specialized in what I needed at the time for the specific place I was in and at the level I was currently operating. He was psychic but chose not to use that label due to the previously long-held, negative connotations that the label sometimes brought. I understood. This man has been instrumental in my awakening. I am forever grateful to him.

So far, to date, I have gone to at least three different psychic/intuitives, a medical intuitive, a dynamic energy healer, a few Reiki practitioners, an iridologist and naturopathic doctor, a past-life and LBL (life between life) hypnotherapist trained by the world-renowned Dr. Michael Newton famous for his spiritual regression techniques that take subjects back to their time in the spirit world, an AFT (Akashic Field Therapy) therapist, and even a horse who gave messages.

I cannot possibly list everything they all told me, as it could literally fill the pages of its own book. However, one poignant session was my LBL hypnotherapy regression. I traveled about an hour from my home. By luck, one of Michael Newton's trained students and practitioners happened to be practicing near my home. I had read all of his books and felt they resonated deeply within.

Prior to the session, I was asked to focus on a question I had. Then the practitioner conducted a guided meditation into deep hypnosis. My question was, *why do I feel so unhappy and bad about myself that I chew my fingers to the point of painful bleeding?* I had the destructive habit for decades.

I had every reason in the world to be happy, and I wasn't. I was retired at the tender age of forty-eight with a sizable pension from my law enforcement career; my children were raised, healthy, and doing well; I had two adorable and healthy granddaughters; I had a loving and supportive soul mate for a partner, with a nice house, two beautiful cars, four dogs ... And yet the sadness was there.

It was undeniable and unsettling.

During my life between lives (LBL) regression, while under hypnosis, I met and was introduced to my main life guide who wanted to bring me to the Hall of Records in order to show me something. I was hesitant, resistant, and wouldn't go with her. She was lovingly coaxing me gently toward the building in my mind's eye. I refused. I ended up going to my Council of Elders instead, where I was given the message that the nature of my soul was gentle and I was doing splendidly on my sojourn and to not fret. I can still see them all clapping soberly in my mind.

And yet, fret I did, and I did it well. Only it isn't something you get accolades for. I was shocked to hear the true nature of my soul. I did not recognize the aspect of myself as gentle. I had spent most of my life covering that up. I had the belief and was taught gentleness gets you nowhere. It is weakness. I was experiencing internal conflict for sure. It felt like I was experiencing a mini identity crisis. I was forced to look at myself in an entirely different light, and it was terrifying. It also made me tremendously angry.

A few days later and once I returned to the comfort of my home, I decided I would try to meditate in order to find out what my guide was trying to show me at the Hall of Records or Akashic Records. I had a sinking suspicion that I might be able to let go enough to access the information while I was alone versus in the company of a professional practitioner who happened to be a virtual stranger, albeit an extremely kind one. After all, I had just met my main guide, and the visual experience was still powerfully with me. I would call on her.

I set my timer for twenty minutes and summoned my main guide as hard as I could and prayed for an answer to the question of what I was so afraid to see in the Akashic Records of my soul during my previous hypnosis.

Within several minutes, I visualized myself as a woman, dressed in a dress, outside on a dirt yard, several hundred years ago, maybe thousands, with my approximately eighteen-month-old son sitting about twenty feet from me, playing with what appeared to be Grecian vases, and I was busy doing something, but I'm not sure what it was. It was insignificant to the scene; I do know that. Suddenly I heard very distinct horse-clipping sounds like a horse on pavement approaching me. I didn't look up because it was a familiar sound at the time. All of a sudden, the man on the horse leaned down and scooped up my son and rode off with him. I intuitively knew in my vision I would never see my son again! I could feel the soul memory and pain as poignantly as if it had just happened. The trauma had been imprinted on my soul.

The next scene was me bowing on my knees to a king, begging him to let me have my son back; you see, I knew— or more applicably could feel—I was a beautiful peasant girl who had a child out of wedlock by a prince who was the king's son. The prince wanted his son but had zero intention of taking me with him. So they stole him from me. Then I felt my conscious mind say, "Don't let that up. It's too painful." My soul replied, "If you don't let this out, you will be sick for the rest of your life!" I needed to release the pain in order to heal it.

Then an overwhelming urge to scream came over me, and I reflexively opened my mouth and screamed this horrible-sounding, guttural, visceral moan/sob/shriek that lasted for the longest time I've ever heard someone scream. I did this for about three minutes or so and envisioned the negative energy coming up from my toes, fingertips, and head, and I threw it out as I screamed. It's such a strange sensation to have two simultaneous thought processes going on. On one hand, you're releasing the vivid emotional memory, and the other saying, "What the heck is going on here? I'm glad I'm alone in my house for this so no one can witness it!"

I did this several times until I basically collapsed back in my chair with a natural calm I had yet to naturally experience in my life. It had to be extremely scary to witness, and I knew then why I didn't want to go the Hall of Records with the LBL hypnotherapist.

This meditation was the first time I had ever been able to recall a past-life memory on my own. I now knew it was possible to retrieve my own past lives if necessary to my growth and healing and was relieved I no longer needed to pay someone $350 in order to guide me. I recognized the child in my meditative memory was the soul of my mother in this life. I had "lost" her (him) again and was facing the pain of lifetimes ago.

On a side note, the mind will produce the cellular memory when the soul is ready to heal that aspect. Do not feel bad or get discouraged if you wish to find out certain information through hypnosis or any other means and it isn't revealed. A couple of things could be going on. First, this is the soul's way of protecting you when you aren't ready to have the information. You may believe you are ready; however, the soul knows much more than the conscious, waking mind does concerning readiness. Secondly, it could be the information is purposely blocked from you so as to not interfere with free will and your soul's progression. Either way, it is for your highest good.

I came to the realization the lesson in that past life that came up was one I had wrestled with in my current life and felt a long-term affinity with—that is, my eons-long desire to go after the shiny, prize partner with disregard as to how I am treated instead of following my authentically gentle-soul nature and tender heart. I had learned in this life to choose the partner who loved me the way I wanted and deserved to be loved. A reciprocal love to the way I loved.

One of the most enlightening sessions I had along my journey to self-awareness was in 2015 with a psychic, medical intuitive. She is extremely gifted, and going to her answered so many questions I had had my entire life and several I didn't even know I had. It was as if the clouds momentarily parted, and I was able to get a glimpse of the entire truth and purpose of my life for the very first time. I was given another huge piece of the puzzle of who I am and why life could seem so hard at times.

During the hour-and-fifteen-minute session I learned about the energetic body and how bungled mine was. The intuitive started out with teaching me that the main body of energy that runs down the center of our body or human bio field is called the Hara Line or Shushumna. This is where the chakras (centers of spiritual power in the body) are located ... all lined up along the main conduit of energy.

What I learned specific to me is I had an energetic blockage in my sacral or second chakra. This chakra is most associated with your emotions and sexuality. It's the "I feel" statement of the self. The sacral chakra dictates how one is supported and whether one feels worthy and valuable. If it isn't open or balanced, there are chances one thinks things such as, *It doesn't make any difference what I do, I'm going to be let down.* Emotions of painful events in life are stored here. There are several physical abnormalities and illnesses that are associated with an unbalanced sacral chakra, such as painful menstrual cycles, low back pain, colon cancer, prostate issues, fibroid cysts, and autoimmune disorders (fibromyalgia). These emotional/energetic toxins build up when our hopes and desires aren't met, and the anger of not being honored at the time as a child end up manifesting later in life if not dealt with.

At any rate, I was told there is a lot of strengthened wiring around my second or sacral chakra from not feeling or knowing I was supported during my childhood. When this blockage occurs and the strengthened wiring grows, one tends to grow a wide body, and no amount of exercise or healthy eating habits can eliminate it until you address the core issue of support.

I've found the main lesson of my life or what I'm learning is to support *myself* and feel my *own worth*. This isn't something that can be obtained from outside the self. We try and try to get outside support and affirmation when, in fact, what we are really searching for is the ability to self-support or to find and connect with the divinity within.

We must learn how to know we are worthy beings and can depend upon ourselves to be acceptable in the world.

The practitioner explained the reason for this growing a wide body is because the body is made to follow the energy. My body had been operating under a childhood survival mechanism for a long time, and it was no longer working for me. It was time for me to get out of my defensive habit pattern of digging my heels in to justify my existence and overexplain why I did what I did or said what I said.

In other words, as soon as I *accept* who I am, *believe* in myself, and *know* I am self-sufficient, the energetic wiring of my body will restructure and naturally unblock my second chakra.

It was time to stop trying to justify my existence and just accept who I am without worrying if anyone gets me or not.

I was told by this gifted medical intuitive that I had the unfortunate (or fortunate depending on how you want to look at it) circumstance of being born early. I have the energetic wiring of the young people ... those born within the last thirty years, from roughly 1985 to present. This energetic system is very different from the old system. She went on to say the old system of structure, rules, boundaries, and limitations was wrestling with the new system, which was run by energy that desires and needs freedom and choice to explore.

I don't naturally possess the wiring system for the culture I was born into.

I was advised I was a path clearer or way show-er. The intuitive medium said I was angry and resentful of rules, cheaters, liars, and all the things that make up the old archaic system of establishment. This made sense because I was never satisfied, and I had no idea why.

Carrying incompatible ideologies and energy systems within me caused a lot of trouble with digestion due to the inevitable conflict that seemed to always present itself as I traveled throughout my daily life. On one hand was my desire to conform to deep-rooted societal and governmental establishment in order to be a good girl. The other one involved my innate, hardwired desire for freedom of choice or my instinctive desire to "stick it to the man" by doing my own thing.

There was never any choice involved or "choosing" my path during my formative years. The old wiring was perfectly okay with that and even allowed me to be successful as an adult both in my career and my personal life.

She explained it like this: If I was a "good girl" and went with the program, I was "screwed." If I did what I wanted, I was "screwed." When I say "screwed," I mean not lovingly supported for my decisions. Everything was always questioned, or I was chastised for being wrong for this or that reason or told I could've done it better this or that way.

The new souls being born want—no, *demand*—choice. The best thing we as their parents and adult supervisors can do for them is to support their choices nonjudgmentally. We should lovingly guide them, but the choices must be theirs. It must be okay if we want them to be empowered, emotionally healthy adults who contribute positively to society. That is what they're coming here for.

The new children are coming here to show us how to live in unconditionally loving peace. They are different. They are of a much higher vibrational frequency. We can all learn from them.

So it seems I came here to punch a few holes and slash a few paths in order to make the path more visible. This is to make way for the new souls and illuminate a new way for the souls living from the old paradigm.

The path-clearer makes way for all those coming behind them. The path gets a little bigger, a little wider, and a little easier over time as it gets worn. She referred to me as an "athlete" and said I was depleted of all my trace minerals. I was fried, Spirit said through her, and had been for about eighteen years. The burning up of trace minerals was from the stress over the many decades of taking what I came here to do so seriously and fighting for my right to exist where and how I chose, all without knowing that was what I was doing. I nearly ran myself into the ground. I never took care of myself physically, emotionally, or spiritually up to this point.

I got so good at my role in the old structure of society that I wrapped myself in bravado and mistakenly honed the ability to level someone who I felt needed it. I've since learned that is no way to behave. I may still have the ability to cut someone quickly with my words, if need be, but I've since learned there isn't any need for it. People are where they are, and it isn't my job to personally orchestrate a hierarchical system of punishment if someone isn't in compliance.

And like my wife, Jean, says, when we're unenlightened, asleep, and know no better, we are all just like little yappy dogs who bark as loudly as we can so people will think we're tougher than we are. It's true. When we're unaware of our true nature and purpose, we feel like little creatures in a big world full of unknowns, and when we become big dogs (awake), we understand we don't have to control our environment in order to survive, so the need to "bark" and/or fight back is diminished or eliminated. We know we will be okay and have faith in our ability to take care of ourselves.

Still, during this reading, I felt vindicated, truly authenticated, for the first time in my life. It was all coming together.

I had never even remotely heard any of these things she was telling me. Yet I could feel the inherent truth in them. Things about my life were beginning to make perfect sense. I periodically wept throughout my session, feeling like I was being "seen" for the first time in fifty years.

My life, up to this point, felt like one incessant battle. But the battle was over, I was told, and I no longer needed to fight for it. I could put my battle weapons away. God was, in essence, saying, "Stand down." The old paradigms of governmental, religious, and business structures were finally being challenged and crumbling.

Now was the time for me to learn to live authentically … from my true gentle essence. I was being called to set and be the example. It was extremely hard for me to drop my defenses and make myself vulnerable. I had always mistaken openness or vulnerability and kindness for weakness.

I still struggle every day with that one.

The new souls coming to earth have been referred to as the indigos, crystal, and/or rainbow children. They choose from a new place called the high-heart or peace chakra, although it's not very "peaceful" right now.

This peace chakra resides in between the heart and throat chakra, just over the thymus gland (a lymphoid gland comprised of two identically sized lobes, located behind the sternum [breastbone] but in front of the heart), is vibrant pink, and is the source from where we make decisions in our lives.

A side note: Although the choice to leave my husband for a woman came from this new high-heart chakra, that place that screams for choice, freedom, and relief from the structural establishment, the old dynamic of conforming to the way it's supposed to be was wrenching at me so strongly I lost nearly thirty pounds in about nine months due to the enormous stress on my system. The mind-body connection was in a constant state of crisis.

This new chakra determines what is good for us personally, not what our parents want for us or what society says we should do or be. It's all about *choice*. What do *you* want to do? It isn't about what your mom, dad, grandma, grandpa, teacher, friend, boyfriend, girlfriend, boss, coworker, neighbor, or any other human being wants you to do. After all, how can anyone outside of you adequately know what is best for you?

The truth is they can't.

I was born and raised in a societal structure without the energetic wiring to support or "fit" into said structure. It created deep conflict within me and consequently forced me to buck the system and do what I wanted, all the while feeling ostracized in order to fulfill my purpose. If everyone said, "Go right," it was a guaranteed way to get me to go left. It was in my nature, I was energetically wired as such, and it was my predetermined job to do so without knowing.

The *rules* dictating the societal culture in the old paradigm are eroding. These so-called rules are being challenged in this new developing system of society, and I found out I came here to assist the facilitation of the beginning stages of shifting our world and societal culture into a more unconditionally loving place to live, choose, experience, and grow.

The old system of energetic wiring is rule based. "A good daughter does this, a good churchgoer does that, a best friend says this, a sister does that, a good employee does this ..." and so on. Remember when I told you I was a good girl and hero? Well, because of my desire to please, my body energetically adapted by growing the old system of wiring in order to fit in, feel supported, and be loved.

Accordingly, I now have two operating systems running simultaneously. There are literally thousands of us walking around with the same issue. The intuitive likened it to running Windows on a Mac. It causes you to feel isolated and disconnected while desperately searching for your tribe. It has taken an enormous toll, and now my physical body is in poor shape.

The young, newer souls want to come in and stress the old dynamic, push the envelope, and change the system. I relate far more to this energy and these people than those of my age. I was told I had to be a part of the old system to be able to change things, to rock the boat. It's like being a mole. Keep rocking the boat.

I now had to get out of my old wiring that I built in order to survive in the old, structured paradigm of obligatory compliance and move into the new one, which is a space of … I don't *have* to do anything; rather I *want* to do this, or I *want* to do that. Don't get me wrong; everything isn't all a bed of roses. It is challenging to switch patterns of behavior when your friends and family remember you interacting one way. Now you're coming from the other direction. One way was making decisions based upon what everyone else wanted/expected, and the new direction is choice driven by what is supportive to the self.

So much was making sense now. It was as if a vast piece of the proverbial puzzle clicked into place during this reading. I just bawled throughout the entire reading. The aha moments were hitting me in waves, and it was overwhelming but in a fantastic way.

I will be forever grateful to the gifted woman for her ability to listen to Spirit, who taught me so much about who I am, why I am here, and the reason for my lifelong internal struggle. I had done a lot of hard work on myself and felt like I was finally allowed to know the truth of who I am and my purpose for being here.

I am not telling you this to toot my own horn but rather to encourage you to keep searching. Keep searching for your answers. Your truth ... the truth of who you are! It's already inside you, but oftentimes it is harder to access when it's your own stuff. Reaching out for assistance is a great tool to get you on the right path.

It has been my experience Spirit will give you more and more answers the longer and harder you strive for self-improvement. However, it will be at a pace you can handle as well.

At the next point in my journey, I was guided to another extremely gifted intuitive after reading her book, *Angel Incarnate—One Birth*. CJ Martes, the author and creator of AFT (Akashic Field Therapy) helps in bringing conscious awareness to the patterns that are blocking a person's full expression.

The Akashic (Sanskrit for sky, ether or space) Records or Field is an energetic library of everything that has happened on earth involving every soul who has inhabited her since time immemorial. I was told she knew I was ready to go to that next level. CJ was guided by Spirit to formulate this therapy and was told at that time only people who were ready to make a big leap or pivot point in their spiritual growth and development would be seeking out her healing modality.

AFT therapy was very deep and involved accessing my personal Akashic Field in order to heal trauma and release old patterns of behavior I was ready to let go of all that was no longer serving my highest good.

I was told I was in a space in my life where I am able to switch from survival into thriving. I am turning the corner, so to speak. I am becoming able to truly be in connection with my true joy, the true love for myself, letting go of some of those limiting patterns that hold me back from stepping into my truth all the way. I'm more able to move with divine will, and things are flowing to be free of the past, to turn the corner.

I was really excited to hear this because I was getting really tired of always *trying* to be this or that. I wanted to actually *be* there. I felt like true happiness and fulfillment were always a day away. I wanted it now. I felt frustrated because I was seemingly working so hard for it, and yet it eluded me. I was trying (here we are with trying again) so hard and felt like I was spinning my wheels.

Maybe this is how the path to enlightenment goes. Maybe I was no different than all the professionals who make it look so effortless. No one really talks about the grind prior to getting there. As if there really is an end to learning about oneself. Rather, in my experience, they all just write books about surefire ways to get *there* and then being *there*. CJ Martes was different. She admitted how hard the path to ascension is.

As part of the AFT session, CJ sends a client sheet identifying Core Traumas with their resultant Core Fear stemming from a Core Belief that have been imprinted into the Akashic Field specific to the individual seeking healing. When a soul takes a body in physical form, it maintains contact with the Akashic Field, specifically its own personal record, and is fed information throughout life on how to act and react in any situation. When there is trauma surrounding specific situations in life, the loop of negative feedback keeps circling to and from you. These energies keep you stuck until you address them.

I had a Core Trauma of *separation* with a Core Fear of "not caring enough" and a Core Belief that "I don't know what to do." She said the growth potential from healing this trauma was to learn *patience*.

The second trauma I had was *neglect* with a fear of "being outcast" and the belief "I cannot be happy." The growth potential for healing these wounds was to become *nurturing*, mostly *self-nurturing*.

I could let myself have imperfections and be happy with them. This was a scary one for me. I couldn't imagine going easy on myself. I had never done it. I knew if I learned to let myself off the proverbial hook, I would allow others the same courtesy, although I was always much harder on myself than I ever was on others in my life.

The third Core Trauma was poverty with a fear of "being pitied" and a belief "other people are stronger/ better than I am." The growth potential was *sustenance/ abundance* or the belief I could have abundance.

It seems I had a past life of abject poverty where people pitied me. I despised it so greatly that it traumatized me deeply, and thus I carried it over lifetimes. We all do this. We carry our trauma imprinted on the Akashic Field, and then it manifests in our physical bodies as sickness, illness, and/or poor behavior.

This therapy is so deep and personal it hits you in the solar plexus. It drew up such visceral emotion I had to process and release over several days. CJ warns ahead of time of the potential for this to dredge up big stuff and gives tools to process the emotion. She created an action statement for me to read aloud for twenty-one days while tapping on my thymus (interestingly, there's that thymus gland again!). This process moves the old energy patterns out and makes room to create new, healthy ones that support the growth potential she cites.

CJ Martes' AFT is an amazing, divinely guided tool to use when you have done a lot of work and you're at the place in life where you're ready to finally let go of what's holding you back and step into the magnificence of all that is you.

I want to share how hard the process of getting *there* actually feels. Supposing, that is, one can actually get *there*. I, like many others, are so caught up in the *there* that I often forget to be *here*. The *there* focuses on the future. The *being* focuses on the present or now. Speaking of being instead of doing, there are entire religions whose foundation is built upon that very notion—the state of *being*. Buddhism is one of them.

Maybe that's the singular purpose of life, the journey of getting there. Or the unfolding process of finding out who you truly are. I'm coming to find it is a lifelong process. The whole point to living life is the journey. It's not the destination. I have always been so focused on the destination (there) that I never enjoyed the journey (being).

I have a tendency to be way too serious.

I'm starting to enjoy the journey now.

Stop *doing* and just *be*. Doesn't it feel good to hear that? If you're anything like me, hearing I should do less is liberating and soothing. Western society teaches we must always be doing something to be worthy. Just bring yourself back to presence when you feel your thoughts drifting toward your to-do list.

I am learning to breathe. Just breathe, deeply. It resets your internal energy centers, giving an overall feeling of well-*being*. Try it! Take three deep breaths inhaling through the nose and exhaling out the mouth. It really works.

I suppose there is a need to explain what path I feel I came here to clear. It is the path to the Golden Age and essentially means the earth is in transformation from third-dimensional to fifth-dimensional existence (like in heaven). The new souls are coming in to assist this transformation. It began on December 21, 2012 or 12/21/12. Yes, the end of the Mayan calendar that everyone thought was the end of the earth, end of days, or the apocalypse.

December 21, 2012 did not signify the beginning of the apocalypse. It indicated the end of an era, the Piscean era, and the beginning of the new millennium or Golden Age or the Age of Aquarius. It represents earth's transcendence to a higher vibrational frequency of truth, like that of the fifth dimension ... or heaven on earth.

This system of duality indicative of the third dimension was used for thousands of years because it cultivated an arena for accelerated expansion and we needed it. However, we have evolved enough that acceleration can be slowed down in order to enable us to exist in physical form in a more loving and mutually supportive way.

Ironically, as the acceleration of growth may decrease, our individual vibration is increasing. As our vibration increases, the need for acceleration diminishes. The majority of us have evolved beyond that requirement.

Individuality and respect for all is the new way of interacting. Loving one another and helping one another grow in the way of one's own choice is the new way. It reminds me of a 1969 song by The 5th Dimension called "The Age of Aquarius." The song was about four decades ahead of its time, and interestingly, it resonated deeply within me at the age of five when the song was released.

Unbeknownst to me at that time, I was carrying the new operating system.

The lyrics to "The Age of Aquarius" are:

... This is the dawning of the Age of Aquarius ...

Harmony and understanding, sympathy and trust abounding

No more falsehoods or derisions, golden living dreams of visions

Mystic crystal revelations and the minds true liberations ...

So, this song by a group called The 5th Dimension precipitated and predicted the earth's ascension from the third dimension where we grow through the experience of polarity or opposites: good versus evil, love versus hate, light versus dark, and so on ... to the fifth dimension or one of growth through love, allowance, choice, acceptance, liberty, truth, and justice for all!

Essentially, I was learning to grow through having the freedom to make my own choices and by having genuine love for my fellow (wo)man.

Since we are no longer going to have to learn through duality, opposites, or negativity, there will be no necessity to expand through good versus evil or light versus dark. The need to become enlightened or ascend through the old structural paradigm of negativity is being replaced. Do as I tell you, follow the leader, don't rock the boat, and be sure to color between the lines or else your "picture" isn't good enough are all phrases that are becoming obsolete. We are growing into a state of allowance. Just allow.

Live and let live! Everyone's "picture" is good enough just the way it is.

Authenticity: Speaking Your Truth

You teach and you heal through your actions.

—New Mexico Indian tribal grandfather, Mimbreno
(channeled by CJ Martes)

Almost every spiritual book talks about being your true self, your authentic essence, or the true you. The reason for this is you cannot live in opposition to your soul and be enlightened. If you do not line up with your soul by speaking and behaving within its authentic form of unconditional love, you will suffer.

The soul is the seat of all truth. It doesn't have the capacity to curb itself in order to please others. There isn't a need. It knows we are all perfect as is.

The soul simply is.

Don't be afraid to be who you are, to speak your truth. The thing about truth is it sits inside each one of us just waiting to be recognized and called upon to be expressed, to be honored, and to be born. However, to bear your personal truth is not an easy task at first.

Early on in life as young infants and toddlers, we naturally express our truth. We have no filter. At birth (and near death), you are as close to Source energy as you'll ever be during your lifetime; hence the term "childlike innocence." It makes sense, as we just came from there (home), the place of unconditional loving energy.

Incidentally, this is why young children have imaginary friends. They are using their innate clairvoyance capabilities and are communicating with spirit energies. Try not to diminish any children who say they see what you cannot see. They aren't making it up. They are speaking their authentic truth; they have yet to learn to hide it in conforming to societal pressure.

Please encourage and support your children and grandchildren to be their authentic selves from birth.

When we are born, we haven't been taught by society and family to curb the truth of who we are in order to conform within the preset guidelines and parameters of society. Unfortunately, oftentimes one's personal truth is not in alignment with that of others in life, so it is kept within and withheld. As time goes on and the truth of who we are is withheld, the essence of who we *really* are gets covered up and lost. Thus, when you do want to recover the true you, it becomes harder and harder to unveil the older we become.

The good news is the real you is never lost forever, as the truth and core of who we are resides within the soul, that part of us that is eternal. Therefore, it patiently waits for us to access it when we are ready to live by it. All that is necessary is the desire to live more authentically (coupled with a lot of hard work). But in my experience, after living covering up my gentle and highly sensitive nature for so long, getting in touch with it was not easy. It takes practice and mindfulness or being present repeatedly until it becomes natural.

I'll tell you a short story of a situation that came to me shortly after I got a sign I was to live more authentically. I had a defragmentation session. Defragmenting is a process intended to address core issues, clear energies that are no longer needed, and retrieve fragmented energies. Another name for this process is called soul retrieval work. The idea behind the process is to put back together pieces of our soul that have been broken off (energies) as a result of negative experiences (trauma) and programming in our current and even past lives. For each intimate relationship you have had and/or trauma you have experienced, a piece of your soul energy is left with that person or in that physical place where the trauma occurred.

When this defragmenting of the soul occurs, it holds us back and/or blocks us from going forward in expansion of the soul and keeps us from the success and abundance intended for us by Source or God.

During my defragmenting session, the first thing that came to the practitioner's sense was I wasn't living my truth. She said, "You're not truly allowing yourself to be authentic in the world; you're still holding back with who you are."

At the time, I told her I was frustrated and confused because I kept hearing this message from various practitioners. I said, "I'm such a straight-shooter," so I felt like I always spoke my truth. She then said, "Speaking your truth, yeah, but what does your soul want to do here?" Bam!

Being authentically you isn't just saying how you feel about certain things; it's about living within each moment, being present and communicating from your soul with regard to how you would like to be seen in the world. A way to assess this is to look closely at each action and each thought in each moment of each day. Do you and your thoughts line up with who you are and how you would like to be seen in the world?

Who are you? What legacy do you want to leave?

I was speaking truths but not coming from a place of love. I was more of a drill sergeant about it. The message was correct, but my delivery was off-putting, and I wondered why people would recoil from me. My soul was screaming at me to be more gentle and loving, yet it was my ego driving the bus. I felt out of control a lot and confused at the constant inner turmoil and battle between my true essence (soul) and my ego. I was mired in guilt and shame for living so contrary to my true gentle essence. I would continuously beat myself up when I was less than loving.

I believe that happened in order to get me to realize that I wasn't acting in accordance with my authentic self. I got tired of feeling bad about "biting people's heads off" or being extremely impatient. I started looking into why I always felt so awful. The soul speaks to you through your emotions. Listen to your emotions and begin to ask yourself why you're feeling the way you are. Trace it back to an original thought or feeling, and you'll find the cause.

I listened to the tape of this session several times until the aha moment came. It was much, much deeper than I had been looking, as is usually the case.

A clear bell was ringing, and I "heard" it.

Back to the story … Having the aha moment cleanly planted in my head from listening to this taped session over and over and even writing it down (transcribing) on paper, I went to wash my car.

It was wintertime, and the roads were full of salt. Along one side of the carwash is a long line of about twelve vacuums where you pull up after the wash. There you can dry your car and vacuum it out if you choose. I was parked and wiping my car down when a minivan pulled right up next to my car. There were several open spots left along the row, but she pulled up right next to me.

I didn't think much about it but maybe a fleeting thought along the lines of, *Hmmm, that's odd. She pulled right next to me when there were spots open, where there would be no car on either side of her, enabling her to maneuver the vacuum hose uninhibited and have all her doors open!* Nevertheless, she chose to park right next to me. As I'm drying, and she's vacuuming, I hear her start to chastise one of her several children. The tone in her voice was so offensive and demeaning it caught my attention.

I normally don't pay much attention to others around in crowded places. I'm too focused on getting out due to my sensitivities of being an empath (one who has the ability to apprehend the mental or emotional state of another individual).

As I looked up to see who she was yelling at so intensely, I saw her pick a winter coat up off of the front seat floorboard and shove it into the lap of her obviously handicapped child who was sitting in the front passenger seat with her head hung in shame.

Apparently, Mom was mad that her child whose arms didn't work normally had let her coat fall down onto the floorboard, getting snow, road debris, and salt on it.

I watched this scene unfold before me and felt a surging rise come up inside to defend this young handicapped girl of about twelve years of age. Normally I would just keep to myself, shoot a disapproving glance, and move on. But you see, I had the statement about not living authentically from who my soul wants to be running through my head, and as the mother pulled her head out of the passenger side door, our eyes met. She gave an embarrassed laugh as she caught me looking at her and realized I had witnessed the whole incident. Instead of looking away, in that split second, I said to her, *Go easy on her* with a gentle, loving, yet serious tone to my voice.

The mother didn't say a word back to me; rather she carried on with the duty of cleaning her car with the reminder from a stranger that she too is a soul who chose her life and circumstances, and maybe she needed that reminder during the inevitable time of frustration in not only raising a child, but one who is handicapped, that she was a loving mother who didn't want to treat her child in that intolerant manner.

And I got to be my authentic self by lovingly and gently reminding a person in the present moment to be their best without the requisite regret of having come on too strongly.

It was a win-win, and I felt it!

It was as if God had sent her to me to show me how to not only speak my truth but to allow myself to be authentic in the world, and he sent me to her as a gentle reminder to be patient and loving with her handicapped daughter.

That's how it works when you're paying attention and being present in each moment. As soon as a realization is made surrounding yourself and the path you've intended for yourself, God steps up to the plate, meets you halfway, and provides an opportunity for the lesson to be realized. After several times, the hope is that the lesson sticks and eventually becomes a natural way of life.

It felt amazingly fulfilling, and I sensed a shift inside that I hadn't felt for years. I was heading toward my next level of expansion. Life sure does become more exciting and meaningful when you live in the now with a more mindful aspect or element of authenticity.

Over time when you fail to speak your truth and to be authentically present, to be the real you, it starts to show up in the body as disease. Yes, *dis-ease* is just as the word says ... one is not at ease with him or herself, and it manifests itself in the body as illness. It's a wake-up call from your soul, spirit, or Source. The message is, "It's time for you to start really looking at yourself and your life and become the more authentic you."

When the heart and mind don't follow the soul, the body protests. The manner in which it can protest is in the form of illness or dis-ease. The human body is an impeccably designed, perfect machine. I've heard it said it is built to last indefinitely, literally. It's not true that we are supposed to physically decline with age. Our bodies have the capability to repeatedly heal themselves. We actually go through the process of healing over and over throughout life. We cut ourself, the blood coagulates and the skin grows back together.

We age because we think we are supposed to age. We expect it. We become ill because our thoughts make us ill. Poor diet and placing items that aren't really food in our systems doesn't help our physical decline. Our expectations in the form of thoughts manifest as sickness or dis-ease. Our society teaches us, "When I'm forty or fifty years old, I'm over the hill, past middle age, and things won't work correctly anymore." Then they don't. Consequently, we begin to physically decline around that time.

A major contributing factor is when you don't live the authentic truth of who you are, day after day, year after year, your heart and soul are aware of it, yet your mind is not. It is the physical body where the disconnect shows or reveals itself. It's kind of like ... *Okay, if you're not going to live authentically empowered and honor the truth of who you are, then I cannot continue to function properly.* It's akin to dumping concrete in a blender and expecting a smoothie. Junk in, junk out. That is why we tend to get sick as we age because the body gets worn out from all the years of trying to run smoothly as the head and mind are working against it.

If you thought your entire life you would live to be 130 years old, and I mean truly believed and knew it to be so, you would. No doubt.

The real spiritual beauty is oftentimes it becomes dis-ease when you have started to become enlightened or conscious of who you really are. I mean ... what's the point of a wake-up call when there currently isn't any ability to wake up. Once the proverbial crack appears and the light can enter, spirit uses illness to make you connect the dots.

When I was consciously asleep and going through the motions of life, giving little regard to anything greater than myself and my surroundings, truly not even being aware that something more existed, I was in optimal health. It wasn't until about fourteen years after getting sober that I developed pre-diabetes and adrenal fatigue from the emotional stress and resultant poor digestion and nutritional deficiencies.

Adrenal fatigue is fairly commonplace during the ascension process, as the high level energies hitting the body put massive amounts of stress on it.

My body was loudly protesting the stress I had put it under for so many years living unconsciously and unauthentically, not to mention eating a diet full of too much sugar and processed food. I don't believe God brings things to us until we are ready. The old adage *if He brings you to it, He'll bring you through it* applies here. I would not have realized I was being nudged to my next greater whole had I not done a sizable amount of spiritual work on myself. Undoubtedly, the pre-diabetes diagnosis would have been perceived as more punishment for not being "good enough."

When mind, body, and soul are clicking on all cylinders, we begin to become whole. To en-whole is to have all aspects of consciousness working together for an individual. The physical, emotional, mental, and energetic bodies all communicate together as one unit and work toward the common goal of your highest good. To do this, we must first align with our true essence or soul self. Becoming whole cannot be completed without first aligning with our true essence. Source wants all the best for us in life. We hold ourselves back from enjoying all the rewards in store for us.

In the words of Carl Jung, "The privilege of a lifetime is to become who you truly are."

Or as Brene' Brown says, "If you trade your authenticity for safety, you may experience the following: anxiety, depression, eating disorders, addiction, rage, blame, resentment and inexplicable grief."

Or from Abraham-Hicks, "Everything is a consequence of your relationship with your inner being."

Throughout my five decades of life, I have experienced nearly all of the above consequences of living inauthentically Brene'speaks of.

At least I was beginning to know why!

Law of Attraction: Manifesting Life

You're so free you can choose bondage.
—Abraham-Hicks
Washington, DC, workshop, April 2016

The phrase *law of attraction* was first coined by philosophers in the late 1800s. It is a general description of cause and effect that goes back to the very start of human existence and has been written about at the heart of many religions and philosophy.

It operates under the maxim *like attracts like*. Basically, by focusing on positive or negative thoughts, a person brings positive or negative experiences into their life. Therefore, if you believe everyone judges you, you will find yourself being judged. If you feel you are good at your job, you will be viewed as being good at your job, and so on.

One of the main regulations or spiritual/universal laws in life is that of free will. We come to earth to learn our lessons and find joy by way of using our free will. It wouldn't be authentic growth for us if an outside party chose for us. In essence, it wouldn't stick, and we would have to keep repeating lessons until we freely chose for ourselves. Oftentimes, that is precisely what happens.

Have you ever had that friend, colleague, or family member that continuously asks you to make decisions for them? What should I wear? How should I cut my hair? Should I change jobs, have another child, move from my house? Should I leave my abusive spouse? Once you stop choosing for them, they may even become angry.

Think of it like this. If you continue to make decisions for them, you are preventing or standing in the way of their potential for growth. These same scenarios will continue to be brought to them until such time they become confident enough to make the choice for themselves. So you really aren't doing them any favors. That is not to say you can't have a conversation with them pointing out the pros and cons of each situation. After all, what are friends for? And besides, if things go horribly wrong, whose fault is it? You don't want it to be yours.

Ultimately though, the decision is theirs and theirs alone to make. Likewise, you have everyday decisions/choices to make that are for you and you alone to make.

I recently heard a great analogy to assist in following your rightful path. If you knock on a proverbial door and it doesn't open, don't find a two-by-four to knock it down; instead, use that same piece of wood to nail the door shut, as the message is it isn't the direction you're supposed to go.

In taking the law of attraction into account ... wherever you vibrate, whatever your thoughts are, however you believe and think ... more of *that* is on its way to you.

It has to be. It's universal law designed to assist in growth. How else would we know where we were (mentally, emotionally, and physically) if our environment didn't mirror it back to us? We might never see or feel the need to change or grow if otherwise. Growth usually begins to sprout once a soul is sick and tired of being sick and tired (insert any situation here). It's about taking responsibility for where you are in life.

What I'm learning is if your life sucks, it's probably your own fault. I don't mean to be cruel, but it's the truth. We are not victims of other people's actions. We allow them. We let it happen in some form or another. If you don't like the circumstances of your life ... change them! No one else has the power. Only you.

Choose positive thoughts, and positivity will manifest in your life.

In the beginning of one's spiritual development, when Spirit throws you a bone and affirms an idea or situation you believe to be true and is healthy, it is like a gift. It compares to that Christmas morning feeling where joy fills you up. This is Spirit's way of enticing you further along. These are the baby steps of your journey to self-awareness and love.

Ideally, we should all be able to gain information about ourselves that is of a positive nature and be able to hold on to it indefinitely; however, the humanness we are experiencing oftentimes interferes with that positive thought, creating self-doubt. It is then that we must regroup and identify the negative thoughts and replace them with positive ones.

CJ Martes, founder of AFT Therapy, says negative thoughts are not the true problem; what we do with them is. Negativity is part of the human condition. Thoughts of a negative nature are going to happen; it's normal. You're human. She also says most people don't realize that nothing has to be permanently stored as originally perceived. Had she not said this, I'm not sure I would have naturally come to that awareness.

The average person has 60,000 thoughts per day. In order to raise your vibrational frequency, you must transmute negative thoughts into positive ones. This is part of the ascension process. As I've previously said, this process is commonly termed enlightenment.

How do you know when you're having a negative thought? CJ articulates you try and track your thoughts as they come throughout the day. It seems like an overwhelming task to say you must track all 60,000-plus thoughts. So go slowly at first. Try to catch one thought and assess it for negative content. If no negativity is inherent in the captured thought, then simply move on to another one.

You're getting the idea about capturing thoughts and looking for negative content. So now what? What do you do when you come across a negative thought? The answer is *nothing*. Just acknowledge it and let it go. Easy enough. Or is it?

CJ taught me the first thought you have does not own you or have dominion over your existence. You can replace negative thoughts about yourself and judgmental thoughts of others with positive ones until it becomes a way of life. Fake it until you make it!

When I first heard this concept, it was like a lightbulb moment. I was assuming that if I had a negative thought, it was too late. I'm committed. I've always been of the opinion that whatever thought is manifested first "wins" or is permanently imprinted as the only option. Kind of a first come, first served philosophy. Or more profoundly, God knew my thought, and now I can't take it back. No take backs. Not true. You can change your negative thoughts, but first you must become aware of the self-talk and intercept it when it's negative and transform it into positive.

You cannot eradicate all thought of a negative nature while in human form; you just learn to transmute them into positive forms once you identify them. You have the power to change them.

Believe me when I say it takes practice, practice, practice, and a lot of it. And here's a little jewel CJ thoughtfully shared during our AFT follow-up conversation: "You're probably going to falter at times, and it is not because you're no good at it; it is because you're a spirit having a human experience." I appreciated the honest transparency.

So don't be so hard on yourself. Keep practicing and know you will fall short every now and then. And it's okay. Forgive yourself as you would a best friend.

The one thing I've noticed about the law of attraction is it is easier to do without emotion. Once emotion is introduced, as in a life experience, it makes it much harder to adhere to. It's hard not to feel emotion about your relationship or money or your job or your health or your home. They say not to focus on your lack of money or it will bring more lack because the universe perceives your thinking about lack as a desire for lack. It doesn't perceive in negatives.

Ostensibly, if your reality is lacking in money yet you train yourself to think like you have money, the universe will notice the discrepancy and bring you money. I know it feels convoluted, but it really does work. You have to train yourself. The other thing I do is have faith money will always be there, and it is. It always finds its way to me. Always. And ... those thoughts keep it coming.

Have you ever had just a little money but decided to spend it anyway on something you really felt you needed or for someone else and then suddenly money shows up at your doorstep by some unforeseen method?

That is the law of attraction! You spent the last little money you had without thinking or worrying about the next batch, and then it came. It has to come. It's universal law. It's almost as if you knew you would be provided for, and you were.

Conversely, the tighter you hold onto money, the more it slips through your fingers. It's true, and it's because your mind-set is ... *I can't spend it because then I won't have any.* Then the universe lines up to bring you more "not having any."

Esther Hicks is a woman who channels a body of enlightened beings in spirit by the name of Abraham. The messages of Abraham-Hicks are based upon the law of attraction (LOA).

I believe Abraham-Hicks to be spiritual geniuses of universal truth. Their message resonates so deeply within.

During a workshop I attended, I took notes of the salient points in their message that day. Please take the time to read each one. Pause and allow the truth of the statement to sink into your soul.

Oftentimes I refer to these little nuggets of truth in order to bring myself back from the *rumble strips* at the side of the road, as Abraham would say.

The following are excerpts taken from the Washington, DC, workshop in 2016:

- Put your intention on what you are desiring, not what you see with your physical senses.
- When you're focused on the absence of what you want, it holds you in a perpetual lack of it.
- Don't compare your idea to your existing reality.
- Find the *feeling* first; then the thing will come.
- A belief is only a thought that you continue to think!

- In each moment, you have a choice or option to make things better or worse for yourself.
- Look for opportunities to break the momentum of that which you are not wanting.
- Focus on the positive things in your life, and the negative will become positive.
- Get a good night's sleep and wake up with a fresh start and positive focus.
- You're here for the joy of being here, not really to learn, but you do.
- Joy puts you in the position to grow.
- Reach for joy!
- You lead through the clarity of your example.
- You come here for growth and expansion.
- Let being happy be more important than being right. Then the universe will open up to you (was a biggie for me).
- Service your happiness first.

We were given homework at the end of the seminar, and it has stuck with me ever since. It stands, for me, as the key to a happy life ...

Notice the correlation between your mood or attitude and your current situation!

When you find yourself hitting on all cylinders in a positive state of mind and things are really going your way, Abraham would say you are in your *vortex* (vortex = vibrational reality).

Gratitude

Gratitude unlocks the fullness of life. It turns
what we have into enough, and more. It turns
denial into acceptance, chaos to order, confusion
to clarity. It can turn a meal into a feast, a
house into a home, a stranger into a friend.

—Melody Beattie

Gratitude is giving thanks. Being grateful. It is also a huge part of enlightenment. If you aren't grateful, then you're more likely angry and bitter. Being angry and bitter disallows growth. It causes you to remain stuck and unmovable. Reminding yourself about what you have and what is good in your life takes the focus off of negativity and puts it in the light of positivity.

Gratitude is a basic tenet of spiritual enlightenment. When you are grateful for your life and all that is in it, you vibrate at a higher frequency, which makes you feel better. When thoughts are positive rather than negative, you feel happier.

I heard once that if anxiety is a part of your daily life, you should journal daily about gratitude. Buy a notebook, label it your gratitude journal, and write daily. You'll be amazed at how much you really are grateful for but don't even realize until you sit down and take the time to write about it.

It feels so good to write about what you're grateful for. It's hard to know what you're grateful for on a deeper scale until you put it in writing and then read it. At first I thought I wouldn't have much to say, as life felt very normal, without a lot going on. I felt as if my journal wouldn't contain much. I was extremely hesitant to begin.

But I was wrong. I was completely wrong. This should have been a little clue I needed more thoughts of gratefulness!

I promise, once you actually sit down to write in your gratitude journal, you will be amazed at how absolutely mood enhancing it is. It is difficult to have negative thoughts about yourself and your current life situation when you're focusing on the gratitude you have for all that is good.

Here is a little excerpt from my first gratitude journal to give you an idea of what it can look like:

Today I am grateful I have a loving wife who is willing to provide for our family by working through personal sickness in order to bring the things to us that make us whole and feel complete. I am grateful for my son's health and the fact he is self-sufficient although he is in another state. He's with a woman who he loves and loves him. For that I am grateful. I am grateful for my daughter, her health, and who keeps in loving contact with me daily and allows me to babysit my beautiful, adorable, and healthy granddaughters. I'm so grateful to be able to be an integral part of their lives and witness their daily growth. I'm grateful for my daughter's mother-in-law who babysits as well so I may have "me" time to work on my spiritual and physical self though meditation, automatic writing, reading, and group attendance. I'm grateful for my dogs that love me and seem happy and content. I enjoy taking loving care of them and seeing their loving little faces and constant quests for love. I too feel that way often. I'm grateful for all my brothers and sisters and nieces and nephews. I'm grateful to my brother who is sober and growing toward Source every day. I love him. I'm grateful to all of my spirit guides who support me daily and love me with no strings attached—unconditionally—just like my wife! Today, I'm grateful for myself and my dedication to becoming a more enlightened human being with a specific purpose. I'm grateful for my intuitive coach and his loving assistance in my journey through his messages. I'm grateful to be of sound health so I can help my daughter and son-in-law paint their new, first home. I'm grateful for the nice, long conversation I recently had with my amazing son. I'm grateful for another happy and healthy day of life. I'm grateful for my beautiful home, my loving wife and kids, and my amazingly adorable and healthy granddaughters. I'm grateful to be sober and able to read in the evenings. I'm happy today, and for that I have gratitude. I'm grateful to be going off my antidepressant medication and feeling strong enough to be okay. I'm grateful our PMI finally fell off of our mortgage and our house payment has reduced. I'm grateful for the patience to wait for it to naturally fall off instead of withdrawing money out of our 401K in order to make it happen sooner. I'm grateful my father is accepting of our help and letting Jean detail his car and that he has the faith in her to do a good job. I'm grateful for the ability for early retirement and that our finances are in order and we don't have a lot of debt. I'm grateful for the beautiful rain after our lawn was aerated and over-seeded two days ago.

The above was taken from the first two days I began my gratitude journal. So you can see, once you sit down and write all you have to be grateful for, it ends up being quite a sizable amount. When you memorialize it by writing it down, you can always go back and read through it when you're feeling low.

Maintaining a state of gratitude is a sure pick-me-up.

When gratitude for life becomes an integral part of your day, it enables you to flow with the river of life. If you don't allow yourself to go with the flow of life, you feel anxious. Something isn't right. It presents like that nagging sensation in the recesses of your mind, never leaving you alone.

You cannot push against the river of life. A river will go on regardless. If you push the river, all you're really doing is creating new tributaries, as the river cannot be stopped. So, I say get in the canoe and ride wherever the river takes you.

As the canoe goes downstream bringing you in contact with the situations and scenarios you previously asked for from God in order to learn the predetermined lessons you've chosen for yourself, you get to make choices. These choices are in the form of daily decisions about whether you want to participate in a particular event or engage a specific individual.

Basically, the river brings you to certain stations, situations, and individuals that serve as signposts in life, and we all have free will as to whether we engage or not. The plan is, hopefully, once you've participated in enough situations that are contra to the truth of *who* you are, you will then begin to choose only those arenas most fitting for you. When this happens, you'll know. You'll feel it. Identifying the feeling of living your purpose and making correct choices for your soul and purpose cannot be taught or adequately explained other than *once you feel it, you know*. We've all had moments along our journey where we knew we were exactly where we were supposed to be, doing what we were supposed to be doing, with whom we were supposed to be doing it.

Once you learn to choose situations, scenarios, and people most in alignment with your true essence, you begin to enhance your life by adding to the overall happiness and wisdom of your soul.

Do not power your way through life by forcing closed doors open (remember the two-by-four analogy). It never leads to your authentic purpose. Go where the ease is. Be water.

Stop trying to fit that square peg in the round hole!

In the words of Caroline Myss, "The goal of becoming a conscious person is not to outwit death, nor even to become immune to disease. The goal is to be able to handle any and all changes in our lives and in our bodies without fear, looking only to absorb the message of truth contained in the change."

And ... "Mastery of the physical self is not the goal of becoming conscious: mastery of the spirit is the goal. The physical world and the physical body serve as the teachers along the way. They are the tools the Spirit uses to learn."

So, instead of continuously asking yourself why—Why does my back ache? Why is my blood sugar borderline, reaching the diabetic markers? Why does my car keep breaking down? Why am I in a toxic or unfulfilling relationship?—use these situations as lessons or indicators to look inward. Find the questions within, and then can you find the answers.

It may be that God/universe/Source is trying to get your attention so you'll look at what may not be best for *you*:

- a car that continuously breaks down when engaged in a long-distance relationship
- airline losing your luggage on your honeymoon
- trying to refinance your home and the call keeps dropping or disconnecting … (True story: I told the man I was starting to get the impression I wasn't supposed to refinance my home. I ignored the signs and went against my gut/instinct/intuition and booked an appraisal anyway. It came in too low, and the refinance didn't go through, and I was out $450!)
- you go for a job interview you may or may not have a deep desire for and cannot find a parking spot in order to make it in time, or your car breaks down on the way, or you get in a fender bender or are pulled over for speeding or a flat tire

All these signs can be attributed to the universe attempting to steer you in the correct direction of your previously well-planned path and purpose for your life. Your job is to pay attention to and be grateful for the signs.

Sometimes the answer is you just needed to start asking yourself the right questions in order to begin (or continue) living a fully conscious life.

Why do you need to live a fully conscious life? For starters, once you've begun to seek answers to life's big questions, the cat is out of the bag, so to speak. The bell has been rung. You can't un-ring the bell. When you become more of a conscious being, you find your purpose with ease due to an increased ability to read the signs and therefore benefit from a more fulfilling life.

The universe doesn't allow you to forget. You can remain still or stagnant, but you can never go backwards or un-re-member.

That is called evolution. Evolve. Keep changing. Keep growing. Keep asking. Keep learning.

Our journey is never over. So relax and enjoy the ride. Why jump out of the canoe and fight against the current and flow of life when you can comfortably stay seated inside the boat and watch life as you go by in a healthy detachment?

Detachment isn't being uncaring, cold, or emotionless. Detachment is letting go of an expected outcome to any relationship or situation and simply responding truthfully in any given moment. Living from the heart and not allowing your brain/ego to run the show. Feel your way!

Once the soul begins to align with the personality, you then flow down the river of life peacefully, uninhibited, and free. When this happens, gratitude is much more easily felt and expressed.

A life lived with gratitude yields happiness.

Have an attitude of gratitude!

Akashic Record

The greatest storehouse of infinite knowledge you will
ever explore awaits you in your Akashic Record.
—Lisa Barnett

The Akasha or Akashic Records is an energetic storage
library of all thought and action of souls during each
incarnation on earth since the beginning of time. It
records the individual nature of us and our relationships
to the universe.

Also termed *The Book of Life*, it can be equated to
the universe's supercomputer system or database. Edgar
Cayce says it is a system that acts as the central storehouse
of all information for every individual who has ever lived
upon the earth. More than just a reservoir of events,
the Akashic Records contain every deed, word, feeling,
thought, and intent that has ever occurred at any time in
the history of the earth world.

Much more than simply a memory storehouse,
however, these Akashic Records are interactive in that
they have a tremendous influence upon our everyday lives,

our relationships, Akashic body, our feelings and belief systems, and the potential realities we draw toward us.

The word Akasha in several ancient texts and Sanskrit most commonly translates into *sky library*. The ancient Tibetans, Egyptians, and some Chinese, Lemurian, and Atlantean cultures had the word Akasha that meant *ether* or *air*.

The Akashic Records can be viewed as God's library of all soul records that incarnate on planet Earth. Each life you've had is recorded in this energetic library of vibration. There are no physical books, per se, although if you want to manifest a book to experience while you consult the Akashic Records, you're more than welcome to do so.

The library is utilized as a place for your life review once you've crossed over or transitioned (death). You and your guides review your life for missed opportunities, resentments, and also triumphs and successes. You can then correlate how this most recent lifetime relates to all of your lives and check your soul's progression.

Accessing your Akashic Records while still experiencing an earthly life brings you to a state of enlightenment by knowing yourself fully. It also activates certain dormant psychic aspects of yourself in order to assist you in changing any aspect you'd like to change while you're still alive. This gives unlimited opportunity and can eliminate the need to be required to reincarnate in order to undo any instance, circumstance, or situation you would like to change.

Accessing your personal Akashic Record can give you the precise information needed in order for your life to become more consciously driven.

What I'm learning is in order to live a more conscious life, to truly step into its essence and wear it as a favorite suit or pair of well-worn pants, making it a part of you,

you must be aware of each moment and make conscious decisions at each of those moments of your life, day by day. As you look back, you'll see a consciously driven life, and before you know it, you'll be living consciously from your soul, conveying your true authentic self in each moment.

We humans tend to complicate things by always looking to the future and how we will be in that moment or the past and how we regret some of those moments. The true joy is in the moment. Happiness is a choice to be made in each moment.

Happiness, peace, and joy can only be found in the present moment. It is a gift; that is why it is called the *present*.

Switch your focus. Look at your life right now. What can you do right now in the present moment to consciously decide to be authentically you? How can you behave or what can you say that aligns you with the essence of your soul, that divine aspect that is within all of us, connecting us to one another?

I believe this is precisely the idea behind the WWJD (What Would Jesus Do) movement around the turn of the century in 2000. There were rubber wristbands with WWJD imprinted on them. The idea is that each time you are presented with a decision, you are to make it from a place of consciousness and ask yourself what Jesus would do. They act as a gentle reminder.

These caught on like wildfire as an attempt to bring people to be cognizant of their everyday decisions in order to live a more Christ-conscious life. Christ consciousness does not mean Jesus the Master of the Christian faith. Rather, it's an aspect of Creator Source; Christ comes from "Chritsus," meaning anointing. It holds the intention of divine compassion, non-judgment, and unconditional love with absolute clarity.

The reality is that we are all one. We come from the same place ... the divine source of all that is. You are an individual spark of divine source energy or God incarnate!

An example of living in the moment and being conscious may be deciding what you're going to eat. The choices are endless, the convenience is readily available, but you want to start treating your body more lovingly because you're realizing what a gift life is and you wish to honor the source of creation by respecting yourself and the vessel you've been given. It's really no different from taking great care of your car by lovingly washing and waxing it. You may feel compelled to choose a salad full of healthy greens and ripe, fresh fruits and vegetables instead of a fast-food burger and fries.

Plant-based foods that grow on a vine or in trees have live enzymes in them. These live enzymes aid enormously in digestion. The gut or intestines are the seat of the emotions. It's most healthy to keep things moving so stagnant energy doesn't have time to turn into dis-ease.

Another example of living in the present or being conscious is when you're having a conversation with a family member, friend, colleague, or coworker and you listen more deeply to their side and try to withhold judgment and hold a more loving and tolerant space for them. Maybe instead of focusing on the negative aspects of life, you could gently point to the positive in the situation or relationship they're speaking about. Withhold your opinion unless asked.

We all want to be heard, to be seen, and to be loved. In my experience, I've found you get what you give. Universal law, law of attraction, or karma dictates what you put out into the world energetically vibrates at a specific frequency, and therefore all things in the form of people, situations, and circumstances of that same vibratory match will find their way back to you, like a boomerang.

Being conscious is about figuring out how to better your life and circumstances through your own actions.

First, you realize there is something amiss in your life; you feel empty, like something is missing. After years, even decades, it begins to dawn on you that you may be a part of the problem. This begins the process of taking responsibility for your life and where you are in it. Start to take inventory of your life, and soon you'll realize some of your everyday decisions are made by rote, sheer habit, without any real thought behind them, based on old programmed beliefs that you no longer even believe. You then begin to realize certain things are not how you would ideally have them if given a choice.

Bingo! There it is. Choice! You have choice in every single matter of your life regarding every circumstance in it. Once this realization hits, you begin to make the choice to live a more authentic life, a more true and accurate reflection of who you are and what you're about.

Making the decision to live your truth invariably comes with the daunting feeling of, how can I do it? How do I undo all the lies I've not only told myself but the universe at large? Lies such as, "Sure I'll coach Little League baseball and love it," or, "Sure I'll pick up your child every day after school without any form of compensation or reciprocation," or, "Yes, I'll coordinate that after-hours project and donate my precious time even though I have a family at home who not only needs me but I need as well."

The *how* is in the moment. Make each and every decision in the moment from a conscious position of ... *will this be a true reflection of my authentic self? Am I being honest and kind and is this really who I am and want to be?*

Do not worry about how you appear to others. Living a conscious life isn't easy at first. There are excruciatingly painful moments when you go from living from personal will to divine will. Being a conscious being, at its core, is really just surrendering to divine will, that part of you that is inside everyone, the divinity within.

Become still enough to hear the instruction in your gut or heart and strong in faith enough to carry it out. Have faith that every instruction is for your highest and best potential growth and being. You will inevitably be led in the direction of your true purpose. All you need is the ability to let go. Really! Really.

Let go of the need to orchestrate your life down to the minute detail and make conscious decisions in each moment one by one, day by day, month by month, year by year, and before you know it, you'll be a fully conscious being.

Slow it down. Here is an example of what I'm talking about:

As I'm writing this part of the book, it is 6:00 a.m., and I've got to get ready to babysit my granddaughters, so I have a decision to make. Do I stop writing so I can take a shower and be fresh for my twenty-month and one-month-old granddaughters, or should I make a good breakfast with greens and fresh berries in order to heal my pre-diabetic body from years of abuse? The old self would have chosen to shower most definitely, but my conscious choice to become healthy and treat myself lovingly and with respect for the divine opportunity to enhance my soul will choose the healthy breakfast so I can be strong enough to play with my grandchildren, as I'm fairly certain they aren't going to give me the "sniff test." However, the twenty-month-old will undoubtedly remember me getting on the floor and playing with her!

That was a conscious choice made in that moment, which served my greater conscious self and desire of being an available mother and grandmother.

As you become more and more spiritually connected to the source of all that is, which I call God, you begin experiencing synchronicities and déjà vu, all pointing to the direction Source will have you go. Remember, they're like signposts on your road map of life.

One such example for me is when I was on Amazon purchasing a book when a suggested reading came up under my purchase. You know how that happens? You purchase something, and then you receive a plethora of like examples enticing you to make another purchase. Anyway, I had been reading many, many spiritual books when this suggested book popped up that really didn't have much to do with the topic of what I had just purchased.

This suggested book was about the Akashic Records and how to access them in order to do automatic writing. Automatic writing, also termed spirit writing, is said to be produced by a spiritual or subconscious agency rather than by the conscious intention of the writer. It is a practice where you set an intention, ask for protection, and call on your spirit guides and or any beings of light in order to channel information and messages from the spirit realm.

Now, I had heard of automatic writing through reading all of Betty Montgomery's books about her journey and how she began to channel spirits from the other side or heaven, who had crossed over. Accordingly, I believed it was possible at the time and wondered if I could do it.

Fast-forward two years, and this unrelated book pops up for me to consider purchasing. I read the little excerpt, and it said it was a step-by-step guide to access the Akashic realm and do automatic writing of your own. I was intrigued and a little baffled when I found myself purchasing such a book. I never believed I would be chosen to be a channel for higher energies to speak through. Nonetheless, on some level, I wanted to be used in that way in order to bring hope, love, joy, freedom, and wisdom to a world so thirsty for something more and new. The universe responded to my desire.

I just knew there was more to life than a nine-to-five job, divorce, illness, addiction, pain, and then death. I mean, what would be the point? Right?

So I read the book and followed the step-by-step guide in how to access my own Akashic Record, said the necessary and requisite prayers, and—boom! It worked! The first time I tried, it worked just as the book said it would. Rather effortlessly I might add. I was shocked, incredulous, honored, humbled, and giddy with excitement along with every other positive emotion.

The whole point of this story is to impart that if I could have a spiritual experience such as this and be shown some of my gifts, then certainly so can you. The mere fact that you're reading this book says you're ready, based upon the title. Maybe you've been well on your way, silently preparing all your life, and just needed or wanted to hear someone else's perspective.

I would like to share some of the wisdom my guides, named The Enlightened Ones (TEO for short), have shared with me. To relay all I've been given would be a whole book.

Early on when I accessed the Akashic realm, I was given some sage advice that was tailor-made for my soul. My essence tended to be excitable to the point of turbulent. I couldn't relax even if I was in the middle of a Zen Buddhist colony surrounded by the most peaceful monks on earth. I always had to be moving; even if I wasn't physically moving, I was mentally or energetically moving, sometimes with no real destination in mind. In hindsight, I now know I was running from myself.

The salient first pieces of knowledge I channeled in the early stages of my automatic writing were truly life changing for me. I had asked, "What is most important for me to know today?" They responded with the following:

> "Just that you can stop this vicious cycle and flush your ego from your earthly lives and still be effective. Listen to your heart, and there is where you shall hear us always. Don't worry so much about what to 'do' today and just 'be.' You're so not very good at that. It's okay! Relax (laughter). You're allowed to not be perfect at all things that exist. Why would the world need to exist if you carried all capability within your own being? When you consider your ego first before your heart and soul, you end up living an empty existence. You want to love and be loved and consistently tried to create that realm in your romantic relationships to no avail. You know now not to force love; it either is or it isn't, on earth. You cannot force or make someone love you; they do or they don't. They can express it or they stop themselves out of fear and rejection of their essence. Love is where we all come from, and we come down to earth to experience the opposite in order to appreciate our own existence and not take it for granted. It's also a way to purify the soul. Like a fire breaks down a molecule to liquid to reform it when it cools to a purer form of itself. Rebirthing process."

Although it may be information you've heard before from outside sources, I guess there is something about connecting with your inner guidance—it allows for a more impactful punch. It's tailor-made for you specifically, always. Receiving messages from Spirit is always custom-made for what your soul most needs at that precise moment in time in order to facilitate your highest growth potential and benefit. It's amazing, and there's always more from where that came.

The only requirement in communicating with the spiritual realm is to believe it is possible. Then you can begin to trust in yourself and all of your untapped potential ability to access the information.

It's like the old axiom: *If you think you can, you're right. If you think you can't, you're right.*

Allinclusivism

Man. Because he sacrifices his health in order to
make money. Then he sacrifices money to recuperate
his health. And then he is so anxious about the
future that he does not enjoy the present; the
result being that he does not live in the present
or the future; he lives as if he is never going to
die, and then dies having never really lived.
—Dalai Lama, when asked what surprised
him most about humanity

I'd like to term a new way of living, *allinclusivism*, where
all are included in abundance. Like socialism only without
the negative connotation that midtwentieth-century media
and politicians have assigned to it.

It would be a system where we all work together
to achieve the same goal. I'm talking about worldwide
togetherness. Spread the wealth across the globe. End
starvation and hunger everywhere. Make it a distant
memory. Render it history.

There is no arguable reason why in today's society with
all the technological advancements and multitrillions of

dollars circulating the globe that 7.5 billion people cannot reach out to each other and help one another. It's really disgraceful that we allow each other to starve to death. What is the purpose in that? We are all one after all. So it's as if you are starving your own soul by letting it continue.

Big business runs the world. That is not a secret. I recently read that the Waltons, who are the founders of Walmart, enjoy profits upwards of $144 billion. It's hard for the average person to understand that kind of money. However, I do understand that if Sam Walton & Co. kept several *billion* each year and gave the rest away, the other several billion could be used to solve world hunger and disease without even remotely negatively impacting the Waltons' quality of life.

What I mean is they wouldn't notice they didn't have it unless they looked at their bank account statement. Everyday things necessary to live like eating, clothing, shelter, entertainment, and so on would still feel and actually be the exact same, regardless of the surplus amount of money stockpiled in their bank account.

As you awaken, the idea of *all are one* or *unity consciousness* becomes a known, and you start to realize the responsibility or duty we have to one another to assist in any way possible. I mean, how much money does one need? How much money can one individual or family spend? How much is enough? How many cars does one person need? You can drive only one at a time. In my opinion, it's gross gluttony the way the top 1 percent live, especially in comparison to the larger majority in the world who live under the level of poverty.

Instead of a monetary incentive to entrepreneurship, we could create an honorary status system. One could be known worldwide from the philanthropic invention or addition to society and be compensated in lifestyle enhancements in direct balance or reflection of how many people benefited from the idea or invention or service. In other words, one would reap compensation in direct proportion and correlation to how much good they infused into society. An energy exchange.

People who did nothing to assist society or their fellow man would quickly see they must participate. Even if their participation looked like that of a homeless person on a crowded city street sharing their gift of music or any other creative expression meant to lift the hearts and brighten the day of those around them. Thank them by providing food and shelter, the bare necessities of life.

In an allinclusive society, each member would be compensated accordingly. Then, say the free spirit ("bum" on the sidewalk) wanted to go to school to learn more about music, say to compose or write, they would get a free education, paid for by the institution's previously graduated students who have made money due to benefiting from their education from said institution. It creates a constant flow of giving back, naturally propelling us forward.

A system like this would naturally support the most intrinsically societally supportive institutions. The more you give, the more you get. You won't get until you give, and giving can be subtle. Think about the inner-city young adult who mentors young, neglected children in the neighborhood. That youngster is doing a great service to humanity for the betterment of society and should be monetarily compensated for it. By doing so, the probability of the mentor seeking money by illegal means would certainly plummet if he or she were compensated monetarily for his/her positive infusion into society in taking on an intrinsic leadership role.

I'm not saying people should be compensated monetarily for helping their neighbor in an act of kindness. I'm simply pointing out that a societal structure of allinclusivism would, by its basic tenets, reward its inhabitants for assisting the greater whole and by its very structure inhibit the self-centered, egoist behavior that characterizes the self-serving society that we find ourselves in today.

Contribution to the greater whole is the goal in an allinclusive society.

The more you put into society that assists the greater whole, the more you would be compensated. The individual gain would be a direct reflection of the good you contributed to the world. Therein lays the incentive.

It's truly an atrocity that as technologically advanced as our society has become, at a relatively quick pace, there is still immense human suffering. We need time and collective creativity to catch up to ourselves.

I recently saw an advertisement from the Congo Rainforest describing just how rapidly humanity is destroying the planet. It said, *the earth is 4.6 billion years old. Scaling to 46 years, humans have been here 4 hours, the industrial revolution began one minute ago, and in that time we've destroyed more than half the world's forests.* Shameful.

Conversely, money is a societal and personal enslaver. The only way out of enslavement is to get rid of money. Instead of having a system of monetary compensation in order to encourage positive input to society, how about we eliminate money altogether? You can almost hear big business, big agriculture, and big pharmacology groaning from here, can't you?

Cue the eye roll.

Then again, in an enlightened and progressive society, money actually isn't a necessity. That's the big lie! Removing money means creating a system of bartering whereby we exchange our services, assistance, help, creative ideas, labor, love, and so on so that we have so much of what we need that we no longer need money to purchase anything. We already have abundance beyond our wildest imaginations through our individual abilities and gifts. This levels the playing field and brings us closer to an egalitarian or equal society.

JK Rowling, the author of the *Harry Potter* series of books, gets it. She recently lost her billionaire status due to giving away most of her money to charity. She feels an obligation as a billionaire to intelligently gift her surplus back to humanity. What an awesome example to society.

It's human nature to demand equality. What better way to achieve that equality than to remove the one thing that separates us? Money.

Here is a great parable to point out the lunacy of using money as an exchange for services or goods:

The Story of the
Magic Hundred-Dollar Bill

A traveling salesman goes into a motel to rent a room. He asks the clerk if he can see the room first in order to make sure it is to his liking. The clerk agrees, handing the salesman the keys to a room. The salesman lays a hundred-dollar bill on the counter as a good faith gesture or deposit.

About this time, the motel clerk notices the butcher across the street and remembers he owes him for the meat he purchased yesterday. The clerk quickly rushes over, thanks him, and hands the butcher the hundred-dollar bill. The butcher thanks him as he leaves.

Next, the plumber enters the butcher shop. This triggers the butcher's memory that he owes him for fixing the burst pipes last week. The butcher hands the plumber the hundred-dollar bill.

The plumber thanks the butcher, drives off, and pulls into the gas station to fill up his truck. He remembers he owes the garage mechanic for fixing his truck recently. The plumber hands the gas station owner the hundred-dollar bill.

The gas station owner leaves the station and sees a prostitute on the side of the road and remembers he owes her for services rendered and gives her the hundred-dollar bill. She thanks him and goes into the motel to pay the clerk for the room she used yesterday.

The prostitute hands the motel clerk the hundred-dollar bill for the room. At that moment, the salesman comes back from looking at the room and hands the keys back to the clerk, saying it just isn't the right fit for him, and he picks up his hundred-dollar bill.

What just happened?

In the words of Michael Tellinger of GIATV, with all the money in the world, our governments still cannot solve all of our millions of problems. However, over a period of eleven years that Tellinger has been talking about a world without money, there are only thirteen frequently asked questions by those who contact him concerning the problems. Not too insurmountable compared to the issues of today regarding money. And of the thirteen "problems" surrounding a world without money, many are merely variations of the same problem.

It really is a simple problem to move from a society driven by money control and capitalism to a society driven by people and their passion for life. We work together in cooperation and collaboration and uplift one another just as the cells in our body do in order to sustain life. It would be beautiful to see us all working together to sustain a society for the greatest benefit of all. Allinclusivism is living in a higher consciousness. It rids us of our fear and removes the separation.

A society without money removes the negative and dark aspects of itself, such as greed, fear, competition, divide and conquer principle, envy, jealousy, crime, hierarchy, gluttony, hoarding, and most importantly hunger. Fear, after all, is the absence or antitheses of love. Darkness is the absence of light.

The right to eat is an inalienable right to life, or at least it should be. We should all ensure it is so. It has always baffled me as to why we as a society would even think about discussing first world problems prior to fixing the most inhumane one of world hunger. Prior to tackling other problems, let's fix the lack of basic survival needs first ... people dying from lack of food and clean water.

Honestly, it's irrational to think anything else even remotely matters prior to fixing human starvation.

If money were not an object, there would no longer be any obstacles to any kind of progress. In a system run on money, the banks decide who gets what and how much. Or, put another way, the top less than 1 percent decide the fate of the rest of the 99+ percent of the population. It's gross imbalance of equitable justice.

Innate equality would not only be born but would thrive. No one person or group of people would be considered better or better off. People would see it wasn't so. A true egalitarian worldwide society with love and compassion for all would prevail. Motivation to act would be taken from money to love.

It's always the money that creates the obstacle or hurdle in all of our lives. Think about it.

Money does nothing; people do everything.

TEEM-mates

All souls are different and they progress
at a different rate ... Every soul is growing
toward perfection and they can choose to follow
that path slowly, quickly or stand still.
—Subject "Naomi," from *The Wisdom of the Soul* by Ian
Lawton, with research assistance by Andy Tomlinson

All my life I've wanted and needed to make things better for everyone. Life is hard enough in the duality of earth having equal parts positive and negative. Every single day brings a little dose of each. At the end of the day, I just want everyone to be happy.

One of my biggest stressors has been the problem of feeling overwhelmed and like I was insignificant to the overall task of bettering the world. How can I do it by myself? I don't know why, but I always felt like it was my duty to fix everything, everyone, including the world at large. Crazy. I know. But as crazy as it was, I still felt compelled from a young age to try.

I remember years ago when I wasn't spiritually awake and I thought nothing, no- thing or action I did mattered in the grand scheme of things. I could do whatever, and it wouldn't impact the whole. I failed to understand the interconnectedness of us all. I was wrong.

Those thoughts come from a belief that we are all separate. We are not all separate. The feeling of separateness is an illusion we buy into when we aren't spiritually aware. We are all connected to each other and to everything. We all come from the same place of All that Is. If I hurt you, I hurt myself and vice versa. In fact, all living things, including plants and animals, are interconnected. We humans are connected to all living things and them to us.

Oftentimes, those people in your life who cause you the most pain and suffering love you the most in spirit. It really helps in order to heal your old wounds to look at them in this light of truth. Once you permit the idea of your enemy actually being your most avid supporter, you allow space for healing, forgiveness, and growth.

You can never relive a portion of your life and make changes. Once it is past, it can only be used as an example of what you wish to try to do again or to never do again.

Living in the present, in each moment as it occurs, allows you to see what your choices are and immediately create that which you desire. Don't spend time worrying about the future because you can't influence it unless you are the only person involved. Each additional party is another possible change that can happen before the future arrives. Living in the past manifests regret. Living in the future manifests anxiety, fear and depression. Living in the present manifests happiness.

Always be aware of the things around you. This gives you the freedom to choose what will affect you. Each and every thing in and around you started as a thought in the mind of the Creator, the One. To Him (and Her) it is all equal. Everything and everyone has equal value and worth.

What I've learned along my journey is that in order to be happier, I must pay attention to the positive rather than the negative. Focus your thoughts, mind, and energies there, on the positive. The more positively focused you remain, the more positivity will be brought to you. You create your reality with your thoughts. Remember the law of attraction? "Thoughts become things ... choose the good ones!" (TUT.com)

Thinking about how to create a better circumstance or environment for everyone can feel like such a daunting task at first. How do you do it? There are approximately 7.5 billion people on the planet, and I'm only one of them. I'm nobody. What I do doesn't matter anyway in the grand scheme of things. Who would listen to me? How much of a difference can one person make, really?

And then over time it hit me. There must be a simple way. Start with the self! Human beings make things much more difficult than they need to be. I started to assimilate all the positive self-help phrases I'd picked up along my path and endeavored to put them to practice. There have been many people who have been sending the powerful message of one person (you) being enough to assist in changing the world.

Here are a few of my favorites:

- "Be the change you wish to see in the world." (Mahatma Gandhi)
- "I alone cannot change the world, but I can cast a stone across the waters to create many ripples." (Mother Teresa)

- "Never doubt that a small group of thoughtful, committed citizens can change the world. Indeed it is the only thing that ever has." (Margaret Mead)
- "Change your thoughts and you change your world." (Norman Vincent Peale)
- "You never change things by fighting the existing reality. To change something, build a new model that makes the existing model obsolete." (R. Buckminster Fuller)

And my satirical favorite ...

- "It is not necessary to change. Survival is not mandatory." (W. Edwards Deming)

So, you see the answer to how to change the world for the better is to change it one person at a time. You. Me. We who strive for positive change in the world are all part of the same team. We must all work together to assist Mother Earth in transitioning into the golden era, one person at a time.

It is more than enough to simply change you and let the rest work itself out. If you worry about yourself by being mindful of the whole of humanity, you become part of the TEEM.

TEEM-mates is an acronym I've created for those who wish to participate in the ascension of Mother Earth and her inhabitants.

Together
Expansive
Energy
Movers

Little by little, over time, I have begun to see that one person, singlehandedly, by him or herself, from the place where he or she is, can and does make a difference. One person *can* change the world. As each part of the whole coming together, all doing their individual parts, the Earth becomes a better place for everyone, and love can then settle and reside in every nook and cranny across the globe. After all, one person doesn't have the power to change another.

Consequently, when we are raising our children and grandchildren, it's incumbent upon us to stand fast in the wisdom of being the change we would like to see in the world.

Invariably, when our child comes home emotionally hurt from a classmate or friend, it is then we must reinforce to the next generation that they cannot change Billy or Johnny or Suzy. We must tell them they have no control over another, but what they do have control of is their reaction to the transgression.

In order to be the change you would like to see in the world, the next step would be to teach the child that the fracture comes from within the other person and to forgive Billy or Johnny or Suzy. It would be the perfect time to explain how much pain a person must be in in order to hurt another in that way.

Besides, I don't know a single soul who doesn't like the idea of being forgiven for a misguided transgression he or she has committed against another. We have all been there and done that.

By handling this situation in this manner, we discontinue the perpetuation of anger, fear, and hatred by introducing compassion and understanding in those painful moments. Teach our children that it isn't about their unworthiness in those moments, rather the perpetrator's own feelings of worthlessness and not being good enough.

An eye for an eye is a statement I have come to strongly disagree with if the expectation is to transcend violence and hatred. That statement perpetuates and keeps us fighting each other, thereby keeping us from growth.

You can count on as fact that if you're walking around breathing and living on the big blue rock in the galaxy, you are admired, touted, and even revered as one of the strongest, toughest foot soldiers that make up the spirit realm. Incarnating on earth is not for the faint at heart. We are the stubborn, strong-minded of the spirit world. We are the warriors of the light.

We are the gladiators who chose the most extreme conditions for the highest and quickest possibility of expansion, not only of our own personal consciousness but that of human consciousness as a whole. In other words, all of humanity's consciousness is tied together via each and every one of us. We are learning to think about and being shown how our individual, daily decisions impact one another.

This is termed unity consciousness, the idea that we all come from the same place, are inherently equal, and are collectively working on the same goal. The separation into individual bodies is merely an illusion of separateness.

If you take a whole pie and cut it up into eight individual pieces, do you not know inherently that your particular piece used to belong to the entire whole of the pie? We are like the pie pieces, each of us fractions or splinters of the whole of Source energy, separately experiencing for the entire whole. What I do affects you and vice versa.

We each simply picked different methods, situations, and aspects to experience so as to add to the completeness of the whole—in order to make the whole more whole, so to speak.

What we do here on earth affects the entire cosmos for eternity. We have the opportunity to assist in elevating the consciousness of humanity as a whole by incarnating on earth at this time (2012+) and individually behaving in such a way as to be representative of the desired whole. In essence, if you take your job seriously (while at the same time having fun), your one life at a time can change history and the future of all, just by living lovingly in the present moment.

It's quantum physics. Here is The Lab Lads', chemists of the future definition of quantum theory: *a theory describing the behavior and interactions of elementary particles or energy states based on the assumptions that energy is subdivided into discrete amounts and that matter possesses wave properties.* I don't profess to know much about quantum physics, but I don't have to in order to hear the truth in the statement. I can feel the truth in it. Can't you?

Have you ever heard the statement "everything is energy"? It's true. Everything is made up of energy. Energy is molecules vibrating at differing speeds; the slower the vibration, the denser the object (table). The higher the vibration, the lighter and less easy to see is the object (spirit realm).

We are *subdivided into discreet amounts* by Source energy breaking itself off into separate parts of itself, commonly known as individual souls, one of which is you, in order to *behave and interact* with one another, all for the purpose of expansion.

Some believe all other conscious life or alien life forms from other dimensions are watching us and how we are doing on earth. Let's make them all proud. Be your best version each day. Don't beat yourself up if you falter occasionally. You are, after all, Source energy having a human experience. You're going to make mistakes and slip on occasion. Just don't use that as a free pass or excuse to *stay* in the negativity.

It can be hard at times.

My ego wants to be first, to be the winner. Yet I intuitively know that it is not necessarily the preferred way of Source. Source or God's natural state is unconditional love. It is nonjudgmental about everything. It's neutral. Like more of an objective overseer of all that is. Nothing is wrong.

The way I see it, Source is the collector of data. It then synthesizes it and uses the information to gain newer insights and awareness of itself for experience, expansion, and potential improvement for all that exists. This process keeps helping itself over time. And as new souls are created by Source, they have the advantage of all who went before them and experienced life incarnate.

The new soul is coming in at a more advanced or higher perspective as a jumping-off point. This is how we are all evolving together. Each part (soul) who inputs into the whole has a role in propelling the whole forward.

The human experience is always striving toward and seeking the next greater whole. So by you striving and gaining your next individual greater whole, you are contributing to the entire whole's expansion to higher awareness, collectively.

The entire point of coming to earth is to experience for Source or God, to grow exponentially by living and bringing all you've experienced back home to the other side (heaven). All the experiences of all the trillions of souls in all the other realms and dimensions, not just earth, return with their specific data of experience and download it into or coalesce it with the source of all that is, thereby generating growth through the collective experience of one another.

Realizing we are all fragments of the greater whole that is the Creator Source of all that is, you can tap into that part of yourself, and you will never feel alone like you did when you were unaware of who you truly are. Look inside for the divine spark that is in and unites everyone. It's that piece that ties us all together.

We are all God because we carry that spark of Him within us. God is a genderless energy carrying the characteristics of both. It is Him and Her simultaneously.

We are all creators. Most of us don't remember who we are and don't believe we have the capability that Source has, and therefore we do not.

Take the self-imposed pressure off. Follow your heart in each moment of your day. It's that simple. You've already been downloaded with a general blueprint of what you came to experience. All the details aren't filled in because you have free will and it's impossible to accurately predict exactness when freewill reigns supreme.

There is no right or wrong in the grand scheme of experience for the divine Source of all that is. It is all necessary for expansion and learning about oneself. Relax. Have fun. It never ends. You never end. You just change.

If you want to shift the consciousness of earth and shape the new world order of freedom, love, and compassion for all that live, you must assist humanity in moving us literally into the golden era, the Age of Aquarius, and do your part in making the shift successful.

It sounds ominous, like a heavy burden, and if you're like me, you may at times feel overwhelmed by the very thought of participating in such a massive job. In fact, you may be saying to yourself, "There is no way to do this by myself. It's such a massive job. How am I going to help expand energy large enough to facilitate change and assist ushering in the golden era, in bringing heaven to earth? I'm only one person."

But, you see, that's all it takes is one person. Each person everywhere across the globe can be that new energy ... that anchor of divine light and love. Think of the earth from a bird's-eye perspective and envision strands of light like gossamer threads wrapped around its circumference, side by side until it completely covers the globe entirely. Now, imagine rotating the earth a quarter turn and new strands of light covering the sphere from that direction in grid-like formation. Each cross point is a center to anchor the light. Those cross points are individuals living on earth who choose to be the light every day ... to be the unconditional love and compassion of the divine. As each individual cross point of light permeates its surroundings, the grid fills in one person at a time. This is exactly *how* to assist in elevating earth's consciousness. See, it's easy!

Be the light from where you are on the grid.

To embody this new way of being, you must live from the new high heart chakra with love and compassion for all that is and all living things, including plants and animals, all while having the freedom of choice to do and be exactly who you are.

Then all you must do, my TEEM-mates, my little soldiers of love, is shift the energy in the area around yourself.

Don't worry about the energy in Guadalajara, Bangladesh, Schenectady, or Toledo. Those areas will take care of themselves as our TEEM grows and grows and grows and so on and so on and so on!

TEEM-mates ... Together Expansive Energy Movers. We can do it, one person at a time. That *one* is you!

Welcome to the TEEM! Thank you for your help.

Summary

The plain fact is that the planet does not need more
successful people. But it does desperately need
more peacemakers, healers, restorers, storytellers,
and lovers of every kind. It needs people who
live well in their places. It needs people of moral
courage willing to join the fight to make the world
habitable and humane. And these qualities have
little to do with success as we have defined it.

—David W. Orr, Ecological Literacy: Educating
Our Children for a Sustainable World

Prior to realizing the simplicity of how to spiritually grow
and assist others to do the same, I searched everywhere for
myself. I paid countless professionals to perform various
healing modalities on me from equally as many different
places, and they all gave me the same message but in
various forms.

The message was basically this: "Your guides
really want you to just take a step and overcome your

fear, personal crisis, and stagnant phase and 'be' the magnificent person you were meant to 'be.'"

Whoa! Help! What? How? That sounds frightening at first and yet simplistic in the end. That is a sure sign of spiritually oriented work—frightening yet simplistic.

I've had Reiki, soul defragmentation, soul retrieval, past-life regression hypnotherapy, life-between-lives regressive hypnotherapy, past-life meditation and hypnosis, psychic readings, tarot reading, mediums, intuitive readings, iridology, and medical intuitive readings, and I've been a member of several spiritual groups, just to name the ones I recall.

Most professionals practicing in spiritual work will admit, if pushed, that they've spent a veritable fortune in money and/or angst over the years searching for their own personal identity in order for expansion and growth. The figure for me is in the thousands over the last seven years, and I'm not done yet.

Getting to know, really know, oneself oftentimes is a long, arduous, and expensive journey. But is it worth the cost? Was it all necessary? Of course it was. Just as it was necessary for Dorothy, the Lion, the Tin Man, and the Scarecrow in *The Wizard of Oz* to experience their respective journeys to discover they were already home and had courage, a heart, and brains.

I began to realize that life, like that story, was built around the characters experiencing a series of lessons to the effect that everyone already possesses the resources they need (such as brains, a heart, and courage) if only they had the self-confidence to express them.

All power resides in all of us, always.

Once you tackle a sticking point within you, you will invariably come to a new one. It's like another rung on the spiral ladder of the enlightened ascension continuum.

Heaven, the spirit world, or the place we call our true "home" is doing the same thing as we do down on earth. As above so below. Humanity's enlightenment is also affecting many other planetary galaxies where souls reside.

By doing the growth and expansion here, we are foot soldiers for the elevation of consciousness on the other side as well. We have elected to come down into the trenches and assist in making it better for all of creation.

Did you know you needed permission to be here on earth? And did you know that permission is only granted if you have the individual ability and desire to contribute to the advancement of the greater whole? You see, by volunteering to incarnate on earth in this special time and being, in essence, approved to do so, you are doing and being enough by simply "being" here and vibrating at your highest potential. That fact alone makes you a TEEM-mate.

Welcome to the TEEM!

So, there's a TEEM, but *why* are we here?

What is the general overall purpose for life? If Source energy remained in spirit form at all times, how could it know itself completely? An eloquent explanation I have found for why souls come to earth is taken from the astute perspective of the Masters of the Spirit World website (www.Mastersofthespiritworld.com), quoted in part here: "When you have nothing to compare, you don't have any experience of the possibilities. Souls are given total freedom of choice to decide whether they want to live in negativity or positivity. The negative aspect of the situation is presented to the soul so it may then choose to continue in the negative or opt for the positive. The duality is a place of judgment controlled by the ego, which judges everything against everything else. It must shun the negative and look toward unconditional love in order to connect to its own essence and Source energy. You are learning what you are (unconditional love), by experiencing what you are not (negativity)."

This is precisely why it is imperative to listen to your inner compass. Emotions are signposts revealing areas you must explore in order to learn, heal, and grow away from negativity. Everything is about choice. As TEEM-mates, we must keep our thoughts of a positive vibration as much as humanly possible. This allows us to raise the vibrational frequency of earth and make it a much more pleasant experience not only for us but for all who come here.

Remember to begin by identifying the vibrational nature of your self-talk. If you want to know what your daily thoughts are made of, look around your life and see what has been manifested.

What is your current experience?

Nothing, I mean *no-thing*, can exist in the physical without it first being a thought in the mind of its creator, you.

As we are all here on earth experiencing for the divine, we began as a thought in the mind of the Creator. Once we complete a life of experiencing for the divine, we start all over again but at an even higher level. Think spiral. The bottom is the start. The top goes on into infinity, indicating we are never really done.

There is always more to experience. Energy cannot be destroyed; it merely changes form. No end exists. So have fun! Create! But do it from a place of love, compassion, and inclusion.

I would like to share some infinite knowledge conveyed via my own automatic writing by my spirit guides, The Enlightened Ones. As a part of a spiritual group, I had posed the question of what our divine purpose was and/or in what direction shall we go?

This was their answer:

"You need and must listen to what we have to tell you today if you are to fulfill what you have already been told you must fulfill. The blueprint is inside, but some continue to get bogged down in the minutiae of outside influences and interferences. Listen and listen closely to our words ... your group meets for the divine purpose of getting the earth up to the level of light necessary to ascend all conscious beings on earth at the moment. Those who choose not to ascend will go home, those who are weary and don't have the strength to ascend will go home, and those who are too much of a distraction and roadblock to the process are being brought home against their will, so to speak. So, you see the earth is being prepped, of sorts, for new energies that are being sent down in columns of light, and those columns of light are activating the veritable DNA of those that do not have the wiring of the new diamond light of love. Those born within the last thirty years have the new wiring automatically, and some have both systems in place ... they possess both systems of energetic ability to hold the amount of information necessary to assist in bringing the consciousness to a level that it will change the experience of earth from three-dimensional to five-dimensional. Mary Magdalene and Yeshuwah (aka Jesus) are foremost in assisting this to be ...

"Those wrestling with the darkness are not to tarry with it anymore. There is not a need to grow through the darkness. This is the energetic imprint of the 'old' way of ascending ... through the darkness, that is. This new way that is programmed into the beings that are being born from 1985 to present are equipped with the ability to grow without having to experience darkness and negativity to be of the light. Choose to be of the light, and that is your reality. Look around your lives, and what you see is a direct reflection of that which you have called to yourself, necessary for growth toward the divine. You are all pieces and parts of Me, the divine, and I no longer wish you to experience mayhem and nasty, dark, black energetic compartments to feel the beauty and divinity of the light.

"We want you to open a school to teach others that going through all of these negative experiences that all of you have previously experienced isn't the required way to ascension. Bring the love. Bring the light. Usher into the earth a sense of love so great that no one will feel alone again.

"You see, we are all love and light, and when we come to the duality of earth, we are in essence forced to forget, and then we must find our way back. Like a maze you've been dropped into and how some find their way out, and others get caught up at various points along the way and never get out and see the light, so to speak. Well, think of it as if the walls of the maze have been removed, and all can see one another as they are—love and light. Now, what one must do is assist one another in their respective journeys and help one another as best you can, and everyone can reach the promised land together as one whole instead of individually, fragmented pieces of that whole.

"It is necessary to say at this point that we don't ever want to impart to you all in *how* your group will pull this off. That is for the group to figure out. But know this ... You will be catalysts in bringing the new way of togetherness in light and love to the forefront of humanity. I've dispatched several, hundreds, thousands of groups from all over the earth to assist in this divine purpose and challenge each and every one of you to the task of assisting me transfer from 3-D darkness to 5-D light. Are you up for it? Do you want to assist in the divine purpose for all?

"You see, I am unable to do it alone. You, all parts of me, have the encoded blueprint inside of you to assist me, the divine, and now it is ultimately your choice as to whether you wish to do it or not. There will be people coming and going throughout this group, but I assure you that the ones who stay in it for long haul are my greatest and finest rewards. You, my dear ones, will be the blessed of the universe, and your faith and assistance will live on into eternity. You all have known this was to come about but have been awaiting instruction in how to and when to move forward.

"Now is the time! Here is the place! And by here, we mean wherever you are at the moment. Thusly, whence you have followed your call to divinity and light and love, you will be given instructions on how to impart it to the world.

"… Live for yourself and lest no others live for you. Go where you wish and let not others have to go with you if they choose not to. Do not judge others where they are at the moment, as all is in the deliciousness of divine timing. Make small steps forward, and I shall provide the big leaps for you. All you must do is believe. Just believe in yourselves, and your purpose will arise from that belief. Then you will know what your purpose is and where to take it and whom to take it to. We shall overcome the stigma of lost consciousness and rise to the occasion of loving one another and assisting one another in the ascension of all. Amen. And so it is. And so it shall be."

Now if you read closely, it sounds like I was channeling God him/herself. I was. It is divine consciousness that is within us all. We all have access to it from the divine point within us. I was told everyone has the ability to consciously connect to the Creator of all that is. This is due to the fact that everyone already carries a piece of Source energy inside. We are made from a slice, sliver, or piece of Source energy. That is what the soul is made of. So, the connection is from within, not without.

I am not special in that way. I just believe; therefore, I Am. Have you ever heard of the Great I Am? Another name for God?

Who or What Is God?

What I've come to believe (know) is that God is not a man, person, or entity sitting up in the clouds looking down on us. Rather, He is more accurately termed "It," an energetic form of pure, unconditionally loving, intelligent, conscious energy possessing both masculine (Father God) and feminine (Mother God) attributes, which we are all a part of, everything is a part of. The part of Source energy (God) that resides within us is more commonly termed the "soul."

The new message for all is that you do not need to, nor have you ever needed to, access God or heaven exclusively by going to church. Church isn't the way. You may go to worship the Creator; however, it is not necessary in order to ascend, be saved, or let into heaven. The other side (heaven) is where you are from, and you are already connected to God as being a part of Him.

You don't need a pass back into your own home. You already possess the key. It has been previously placed within you.

So, in closing, I would like to impart all the deep wisdom I've learned along my continuing journey. I want to leave you with a definite method of exercise you can do daily to lift not only your own life but that of the entire globe and arguably the universe at large.

Now, get ready! Do you have a pen and paper? It's huge, it's powerful, and it's a guaranteed, surefire formula for positive change.

The secret, if there is one, is there is no secret!

The biggest thing I have learned so far along my journey is there's no mountaintop you're required to climb, no program you must purchase, learn, and apply as often as you can remember. There aren't any gurus you have to go in search of, no end-all workshop you must regularly attend, no perfect YouTube channel you must subscribe to, no perfect book that is one size fits all.

The truth is there is no esoteric secret that eludes only you but is given to seemingly everyone else around you. When in doubt, let the universe decide.

There are no real instructions of standing on your head for 46.5 minutes at the full moon while doing a quarter pivot turn as you stick your tongue out and hold it facing east, all while chanting your favorite mantra, to bring about your personal enlightenment.

You'll find along your journey that everybody is out there peddling their product, pushing their program, and saturating the system with how-to tutorials, and sometimes all that gets accomplished is the feeling of overwhelm. At the end of the day, there isn't one program or exercise or system of knowledge that is the end-all for everyone.

We are all different. That is by intelligent design. We do not all respond to the same healing modality, nor should we. There are essentially as many pathways to ascension back toward the Creator as there are people populating Mother Earth.

That is a salient point or more of an accurate way to describe spiritual enlightenment/ascension worth stressing ... the path we seek isn't *to* the Creator, as if we aren't from Him. Rather, the pathway is more appropriately termed a *return to* Him.

My perspective is we all came from Him, and life is about being cast into a situation with no memory of your true essence and seeing if you can find your way home with the divine internal homing device that was previously given to you. Rather, the process of remembering—or, putting back the pieces (re-member) of your memory.

Pick the modalities and/or tools best suited to you and your needs. None is greater or lesser than the next. Ultimately, it's your choice as to what resonates and feels right. We make it harder than it is. Sit still with yourself and *feel* for the answers. They will come.

Begin by meditating for fifteen minutes every day. Prior to setting your timer, ask for clarity of your purpose by setting an intention to find it. The answers within will begin to reveal themselves to you. It's a process.

If perhaps there is no answer at times, that is the answer! Maybe you are not supposed to be expending energy in that specific arena. Perhaps it's not for you. Or it's not in divine timing for you to know at the moment. That's okay; it just means the place where your energy is needed will be coming to you. Relax, trust, and *allow* your path to reveal itself to you in the time it is meant to.

However, you need to be available to and for it, and if you're caught up messing around in an area not for you, you will miss the opportunity that is just right for you. Remember to remain present. Stay grounded.

Becoming a spiritual, consciously driven, enlightened human only occurs when you slow down and decide it is time. When you begin listening to your heart, and no one and nothing else, only then will the preplanned blueprint for your personally tailored life begin to emerge and start speaking to you. When this occurs, you are living your life with purpose. In the words of Teal Swan, "All spiritual practice is a process of unveiling the true self."

Another point worth mentioning is not a lot of spiritual practitioners, healers, and the like will tell you that they too struggle with being human. It's the good ones, in my opinion, who admit to their clients that the process is lifelong and ongoing with pitfalls and dry spells. There can be times where your guides seemingly fall off the face of the earth. Some practitioners fail to tell you it happens for a very meaningful reason, that it indicates a time of accelerated growth. That the reason your guides pull back for a while is in order to let you test your wings by relying on your inner voice.

Many spiritual teachers would rather come from a place of (ego) having attained perfect ascension, and now they are bringing it to you instead of transparent honesty, admitting they too have bad days where they aren't acting like an enlightened being and nothing is working.

In the beginning of my journey, I kept beating myself up for not *being there* after I had mentally learned something. I now understand there is an undetermined integration time period that follows learning new lessons and putting them into daily practice. My self-flagellating practice demanded I do "it" perfectly as soon as I realized the right way to *be*.

The truth is the integration period varies with each person, lesson, or realization and can take years (lifetimes) before you're able to actually live it or put it into practice. Hence the reason we keep coming back. It's okay. You're not alone in that. Keep plugging away, knowing you will falter at times. That's the reality of it. Realizing I shouldn't expect to arrive at a designated place of spiritual Zen and never falter really took the pressure off.

Please don't believe that becoming enlightened is a destination you will attain and then never look back to the days of being asleep. Don't do that to yourself. It is a lifelong journey rather than a final destination. We all have moments of getting caught up in the mire of our past ghosts and demons. Our *isms* rear their ugly heads from time to time. Don't feel bad. Don't hang onto it either. Know you are forgiven.

The goal is to get to a point where the occasional slip is the exception rather than the norm.

You are a magnificent soul who happens to be having a human experience. The whole point of incarnating into a physical form is to learn and expand. Perfection is neither the agenda nor the goal.

Forgive yourself.

If you're constantly expecting perfection from yourself and others, happiness will forever elude you. Don't hunker down in avoidance of the inevitable bad day and resultant negative emotions that typically accompany it. *Allow* the emotions to pass through you. Don't resist them, for what you resist persists. Remember, negative emotions are a part of the human experience. Embrace them when they show up. Thank them for serving you. Then let them go. Turn them over to Source for transmutation to love.

Remember to just *be*. Just love. And all will be brought to you that your soul wishes to learn for its highest good, finest evolution, and greatest expansion.

Always remember to take the little steps and know Source will provide the big leaps. Allow the process. Let go and allow. You are enough!

And when those inevitable and overwhelming feelings of the stress of human life invariably hit, speak to yourself.

Maybe you can adopt the mantra I use: *Just breathe. Simply be. Allow. I am enough! Be water.*

Water takes the path of least resistance. It goes with the flow. Water knows no obstacle it cannot triumph over, through, or around. Just *breathe* deeply and say the mantra three times when you're feeling stressed or anxious and see how quickly the anxiety dissipates.

Try it! No really, I mean right now. Try it.

What I'm learning along my journey is the greatest, most effective way to change the world for the better is to change myself. That idea is a lot less daunting and attainable than trying to fix or change the world.

Be the change you wish to see in the world. Become your greatest and authentic version by bringing your *inner out!*

About the Author

Stephanie Klumpp is a retired sheriff's deputy who attained the rank of major. Since her retirement in 2012, she has been on a spiritual journey in order to connect with the more sensitive parts of herself that having a career in law enforcement didn't support. Stephanie lives in Columbus, Ohio with her wife, Jean Neal. Together they have three adult children and six grandchildren. Stephanie part-time babysits the two youngest girls.

Printed in the United States
By Bookmasters